Simon Edwards

Quantum Computing

and

Modern Cryptography

for Beginners

A Complete - 2 in 1 - Guide
Discover History, Features, Developments and Applications of
New Quantum Computers
and Secrets of Modern Cryptography

Copyright © 2020 publishing.

All rights reserved.

Author: Simon Edwards

No part of this publication may be reproduced, distributed or transmitted in any form or by any means, including photocopying recording or other electronic or mechanical methods or by any information storage and retrieval system without the prior written permission of the publisher, except in the case of brief quotation embodies in critical reviews and certain other non-commercial uses permitted by copyright law.

Table of Contents "Quantum Computing"

Introduction

What is Quantum Computing?

Are Quantum Computers a Reality or Just a Scientists Dream?

Why Quantum Computing?

How Quantum Computers Will Work

The Future Is Quantum

Quantum Mechanics To Interpret Or Not To Interpret

The Adiabatic Quantum Computing Model

Quantum Logic

Scientists Hint at Smartphone – Sized Quantum Computers

Is Quantum Computing Closer Than We Thought?

Qubits and Quantum Memory

Another Hardware Alternative for ML and AI: Quantum Computing

Quantum Search

Simon's algorithm: How it works

Quantum Computing and Healthcare Technology

A New Era in Super-Computing?

Limitations Of Quantum Computing

Quantum Reenactment

Quantum Teleportation And Quantum Theory Of Information

Thermodynamics Of Quantum Computation

Test Realization of Quantum Computer

Future Directions of Quantum Computing

Table of Contents "Modern Cryptography"

Introduction

What is Quantum Computing?

Are Quantum Computers a Reality or Just a Scientists Dream?

Why Quantum Computing?

How Quantum Computers Will Work

The Future Is Quantum

Quantum Mechanics To Interpret Or Not To Interpret

The Adiabatic Quantum Computing Model

Quantum Logic

Scientists Hint at Smartphone – Sized Quantum Computers

Is Quantum Computing Closer Than We Thought?

Qubits and Quantum Memory

Another Hardware Alternative for ML and AI: Quantum Computing

Quantum Search

Simon's algorithm: How it works

Quantum Computing and Healthcare Technology

A New Era in Super-Computing?

Limitations Of Quantum Computing

Quantum Reenactment

Quantum Teleportation And Quantum Theory Of Information

Thermodynamics Of Quantum Computation

Test Realization of Quantum Computer

Future Directions of Quantum Computing

Simon Edwards

Quantum Computing

for Beginners

A Complete Guide to Discover
History, Features, Developments and Applications of New
Quantum Computers that will
Revolutionize the World

Copyright © 2020 publishing.

All rights reserved.

Author: Simon Edwards

No part of this publication may be reproduced, distributed or transmitted in any form or by any means, including photocopying recording or other electronic or mechanical methods or by any information storage and retrieval system without the prior written permission of the publisher, except in the case of brief quotation embodies in critical reviews and certain other non-commercial uses permitted by copyright law.

Introduction

The intensity of quantum computing depends on a few marvels and laws of the quantum world that are on a very basic level different from those one experiences in traditional computing complex likelihood amplitudes quantum impedance quantum parallelism quantum trap and the unitarity of quantum evolution. In request to comprehend these highlights and to utilize them for the plan of quantum algorithms systems and processors one needs to comprehend a few fundamental standards which quantum mechanics depends on just as the rudiments of Hilbert space formalism that speaks to the numerical structure utilized in quantum mechanics.

The section begins with an analysis of the present enthusiasm for quantum computing It at that point discusses the primary scholarly obstructions that must be defeated to make a vision of the quantum computer a significant test to current science and technology The essential and specie highlights of quantum computing are first presented by a comparison of randomized computing and quantum computing A prologue to quantum wonders is done in three phases.

First a few old style and comparative quantum tests are analyzed This is trailed by Hilbert space nuts and bolts and by an introduction of the basic standards of quantum mechanics and the components of old style reversible computing.

What is Quantum Computing? Quantum Computing utilizes quantum mechanical properties to express and control data as quantum bits or qubits. Through explicit properties from quantum material science, a quantum computer can work on an exponentially enormous computational space at a cost that scales just polynomial with the necessary assets. Algorithms that can be fittingly actualized on a quantum computer can offer huge potential speedups here and there even exponential speedups over the best present classical methodologies.

Quantum Computing along these lines has the potential for speedups that are sufficiently huge to make already recalcitrant problems tractable. For example, on a classical computer, it would take quadrillions of years to discover the ground state vitality of an enormous atomic complex to high precision or to split the encryption that verifies web traffic and bitcoin wallets.

On a quantum computer, contingent upon the clock-speed of the gadget, these problems can possibly be solved in no time flat or even seconds.

The Inflection Point: Why now?

The scholarly foundations of QC return a very long time to pioneers, for example, Richard Feynman who thought about the principal trouble of mimicking quantum frameworks and "turned the issue around" by proposing to utilize quantum mechanics itself as a basis for actualizing another sort of computer fit for taking care of such problems .In spite of the fact that the fundamental hypothetical supporting of Quantum Computing has been around for quite a while, it took until the previous 5 years to carry the field to an expression point: presently little and middle of the road scale machines are being worked in different labs, in the scholarly community and industry[7][8]. Reskill has coined[9] the expression Noisy Intermediate-Scale Quantum (NISQ) to allude to the class of machines we are assembling as of now and for a long time to come, with 20-1000 qubits.

What is Quantum Computing?

Classical computers, the thoughtful we utilize each day, use memory made up of bits. Bits speak to possibly one or zero; on or off. Everything computers do, from messing around to sending an email, originates from controlling those and zeros.

A quantum PC is another kind of PC that uses the irregular properties of quantum material science to solve problems that are unthinkable for standard computers. They do this by utilizing qubits rather than bits. Like bits, qubits can speak to a one or zero. What makes them extraordinary is that a qubit can be one, zero, or a superposition of both. That implies that a qubit can be both one and zero simultaneously, making quantum computers exponentially more dominant than their ordinary partners.

By utilizing superposition, quantum computers can solve problems that would be unthinkable or take a considerable number of years to finish. Quantum computers drastically outflank old-style computers in counts, including enormous quantities of similarly potential arrangements.

Because of their quality at dissecting mixes, quantum computers will likely be applied to breaking codes and streamlining complex frameworks. Researchers likewise expect that quantum computers will have the option to precisely display occasions at the sub-atomic scale, giving a useful asset to science, science, and material science research.

Superposition is incredible, secretive, and fragile. The most significant boundary to building ultimately working quantum computers is that qubits must be held in a super-cooled, disconnected state, or they decohere and lose their quantum "enchantment."

Quantum computers are sitting at the edge of common sense. Engineers have effectively developed working quantum computers; however, so far have been not able to get enough qubits working simultaneously to understand their maximum capacity – yet the guarantee of that potential has researchers everywhere throughout the world chipping away at making quantum computing one of the characterizing advances of the 21st century.

Envision a computer whose memory is exponentially more significant than its apparent physical size; a computer that can control an exponential arrangement of sources of info at the same time; a computer that registers in a twilight zone of the room. You would think about a quantum computer. Generally, few and fundamental ideas from quantum mechanics are expected to make quantum computers a plausibility. The nuance has been in figuring out how to control these ideas. Is such a computer a certainty, or will it be too hard even to consider building?

By the abnormal laws of quantum mechanics, Folger, a senior editorial manager at Discover, noticed that; an electron, proton, or other subatomic molecule is "in more than each spot in turn," since singular particles act like waves, these better places are various states that an iota can exist in all the while.

What's the severe deal about quantum computing? Envision you were in a massive place of business, and you needed to recover a portfolio left on a work area picked aimlessly in one of several workplaces. Similarly, that you would need to stroll through the structure, opening entryways each in turn to discover the folder case, a customary computer needs to clear its path through long strings of 1's and 0's until it lands at the appropriate response. Be that as it may, imagine a scenario whereas opposed to looking without anyone else, you could immediately make the same number of duplicates of yourself as there were rooms in the structure every one of the clones could at the same time look in every one of the workplaces, and the one that finds the folder case turns into the genuine you, the rest disappear. - (David Freeman, discover)

David Deutsch, a physicist at Oxford University, contended that it might be conceivable to manufacture an incredibly ground-breaking computer dependent on this alternative reality. In 1994, Peter Shor, a mathematician at AT&T Bell Laboratories in New Jersey, demonstrated that, in principle, at any rate, an out and out quantum computer could factor even the most significant numbers in a moment or two; an accomplishment unimaginable for even the quickest ordinary computer. An episode of speculations and discussions of the probability of building a quantum computer presently saturates itself, however, out the quantum fields of innovation and research.

Its underlying foundations can be followed back to 1981 when Richard Feynman noticed that physicists consistently appear to run into computational problems when they attempt to recreate a framework in which quantum mechanics would happen. The computations, including the conduct of molecules, electrons, or photons, require an enormous measure of time on modern computers. In 1985 in Oxford England, the first depiction of how a quantum computer may function surfaced with David Deutsch's hypotheses. The new gadget would not exclusively have the option to outperform the modern computers in speed, yet also, could play out some legitimate tasks that conventional ones proved unable.

This research started investigating developing a gadget, and with the thumbs up and extra subsidizing of AT&T Bell Laboratories in Murray Hill, New Jersey, another individual from the group was included. Subside Shor discovered that quantum calculation could extraordinarily speed considering of whole numbers. It's something other than a stage in small scale computing innovation, and it could offer bits of knowledge into certifiable applications, for example, cryptography.

"There is an expectation toward the finish of the passage that quantum computers may one day become a reality," says Gilles Brassard of the University of Montreal. Quantum Mechanics give a sudden clearness in the depiction of the conduct of particles, electrons, and photons on the minute levels. Even though this data isn't material in ordinary family unit utilizes it does unquestionably apply to each association of issue that we can see, the genuine advantages of this information are merely starting to show themselves.

In our computers, circuit sheets are planned with the goal that a one or a 0 is spoken to by varying measures of power, the result of one plausibility has no impact on the other. In any case, an issue arises when quantum speculations are presented, the results originate from a solitary bit of equipment existing in two separate substances, and these realities cover each other influencing the two effects on the double. These problems can probably get the best quality of the new computer; nonetheless, if it is conceivable to program the results in such a manner along these lines, that adverse impacts counterbalance themselves while the positive ones fortify one another.

This quantum framework must have the option to program the condition into it, confirm it's the calculation, and concentrate the outcomes. A few potential structures have been taken a gander at by researchers, one of which includes utilizing electrons, molecules, or particles caught within attractive fields, converging lasers would then be used to energize the bound particles to the correct wavelength and a subsequent time to reestablish the particles to their ground state. A succession of heartbeats could be utilized to exhibit the particles into an example usable in our arrangement of conditions.

Another plausibility by Seth Lloyd of MIT proposed utilizing natural metallic polymers (one-dimensional particles made of rehashing iotas). The vitality conditions of a given molecule would be controlled by its connection with neighboring iotas in the chain. Laser heartbeats could be utilized to send flags down the polymer chain, and the two closures would make two individual vitality states.

A third proposition was to supplant the natural atoms with gems wherein data would be put away in the precious stones in specific frequencies that could be prepared with extra heartbeats. The nuclear cores, turning in both of two states (clockwise or counterclockwise), could be modified with a tip of a nuclear magnifying lens, either "perusing" it's surface or changing it, which obviously would be "expressing" some portion of data stockpiling. "Monotonous movements of the tip, you could, in the long run, work out any ideal rationale circuit, " DiVincenzo said.

This force includes some significant pitfalls, be that as it may, in that these states would need to remain isolated from everything, including a wanderer photon. These outside impacts would gather, making the stray framework track, and it could even pivot and wind up moving in reverse, causing regular mistakes. To prevent this from framing, new hypotheses have arisen to conquer this.

One path is to keep the calculations moderately short to lessen odds of blunder; another is to reestablished repetitive duplicates of the information on discrete machines and take the standard (method) of the appropriate responses.

This would, without a doubt, surrender any preferences to the quantum computer. Thus AT&T Bell Laboratories have created a mistake amendment strategy in which the quantum bit of information would be encoded in one of nine quantum bits. On the off chance that one of the nine were lost, it would, at that point, be conceivable to recoup the information from what data got through. This would be the ensured position that the quantum state would enter before being transmitted. Additionally, since the conditions of the iotas exist in two countries, if one somehow happened to be tainted. The health of the molecule could be resolved basically by watching the far edge of the particle since each side contains the definite inverse extremity.

The entryways that would transmit the data are what is, for the most part, centered around by researchers today, this single quantum rationale door and its plan of segments to play out a specific activity. One such entryway could control the change from a 1 to a 0 and back, while another could take two bits and make the outcome 0 if both are the equivalent, one is unique.

These entryways would be lines of particles held in an attractive snare or single molecules going through microwave holes. This single door could be developed inside the following year or two, yet a legitimate computer must have a great many entryways to get down to earth. Tycho Sleator of NYU and Harald Weinfurter of UIA take a gander at the quantum rationale entryways as straightforward strides towards making a quantum rationale arrange.

These systems would nevertheless be columns of entryways collaborating. Laser bars sparkling on particles cause progress starting with one quantum state then onto the next which can adjust the sort of aggregate movement conceivable in the exhibit; thus, a particular frequency of light could be utilized to control the associations between the particles. One name given to these clusters has been named "quantum-dab exhibits" in that the individual electrons would be kept to the quantum-dab structures, encoding data to perform scientific activities from straightforward expansion to the figuring of those whole numbers.

The "quantum-speck" structures would be based upon propels, really taking the shape of little semiconductor boxes, whose dividers keep the electrons restricted to the small district of material, another approach to control how data is prepared. Craig Lent, the primary researcher of the undertaking, base this on a unit consisting of five quantum dabs, one in the inside and four, and at the parts of the bargains, electrons would be burrowed between any of the two locales.

Hanging these together would make the rationale circuits that the new quantum computer would require. The distance would be adequate to make "paired wires" made of columns of these units, flipping the state toward one side, creating a chain response flip every one of the groups states down along the wire, much like the present dominoes transmit latency. Hypothesis on the effect of such innovation has been discussed and imagined for a considerable length of time.

In the contending focuses, the point that its possible capacity damage could be that the computational speed would have the option to foil any endeavors at security, mainly the now NSA's information encryption standard would be futile as the calculation would be a slight issue to such a machine. On the last part, this false reality initially showed up in the TV show Quantum Leap, where this innovation turns out to be promptly clear when Ziggy - the parallel half breed computer that he has planned and modified - is referenced, the abilities of a quantum computer reflect that of the show's crossover computer.

What Are Quantum Computing and Quantum Computers?

A significant part of the 21st century information on customer gadgets and profoundly cutting edge innovations depends on man's developing comprehension of Quantum Mechanics. This generally new advancement in material science manages the subatomic world, of particles and circles scientists named with Greek and Latin letters, and of the field's plan to control, foresee and control such universes that individuals can never observe yet exist. It is against hypothetical material science work. Don't bother (or if nothing else put in a safe spot) the ebb and flow Holy Grail of science, the general bound together hypothesis or string hypothesis, on the grounds that the clashing, befuddling and apparently dice-playing Quantum Mechanics gives scientists the research and application for the improvement of computer science, data technology and numerous different fields of designing. At any rate it has certifiable application dissimilar to the string hypothesis. What's more, truly, even the present promotion on contact screen gadgets includes the subatomic universes.

A little clarification of the Quantum mechanics first. In the Quantum world, everything is a bedlam; there is nothing that can be anticipated in subatomic level, in contrast to the physical world. Obviously they can be controlled and controlled for genuine application. One such innovative use of the shakers player Quantum mechanics is the Quantum computer/computing. They are not normal for the transistor-based conventional computers.

With a Quantum computer, the utilization of subatomic particles and their wonders, for example, superposition and snare, are conceivable; hence making the 'dice-playing' unsurprising and controllable. Scientists would now be able to perform activities on quantum information; and the essential thought here is that quantum properties can speak to information and be worked upon. It is first idea out by physicist Alan Turing in 1936 and conjectured the widespread quantum computer, otherwise called the quantum Turing machine. It won't be less right to state than rather than customary bits and bytes, Quantum computers use particles of all the Greek and Latin letter set.

In any case, near a century henceforth, quantum computer is still in its newborn child stages. Yet, it has stopped to be just a subject of hypothetical research, and is starting to come to fruition in applications and tests. Calculations for such trials are done on amounts of quantum bits (qubits for short). And at the same time governments and research offices are presently supporting the advancement of Quantum computers due to its potential for a much increasingly incredible, exact and quicker counts and calculations. Military men will clearly like its suggestions.

Generally, a Quantum computer is an amazing computer. Its memory can be exponentially bigger, for example, in a large number offer a bytes (scientists likely don't have a name yet for it); however just with an insignificant size, say a card or a microchip. It can compute a huge number of data sources all the while and significantly quicker and better. It will without a doubt have extraordinary ramifications on everyday living, if Quantum computers are mass-delivered soon. Also, it won't be less right to state that Quantum computing is the eventual fate of all present-day computers. In any case, the truth will surface eventually if this exceptionally cutting edge innovation is too hard to even consider building.

For what reason do these quantum impacts matter?

Above all else, they're interesting. Far better, they'll be incredibly valuable to the future of computing and correspondences technology.

Because of superposition and entrapment, a quantum computer can process countless estimations at the same time. Consider it this way: while a classical computer works with ones and zeros, a quantum computer will have the upside of utilizing ones, zeros and "superpositions" of ones and zeros. Certain troublesome undertakings that have for some time been thought unimaginable (or "recalcitrant") for classical computers will be accomplished rapidly and productively by a quantum computer.

What can a quantum computer do that a classical computer can't?

Calculating huge numbers, first off. Increasing two enormous numbers is simple for any computer. Be that as it may, figuring the components of an exceptionally huge (state, 500-digit) number, then again, is viewed as incomprehensible for any classical computer. In 1994, a mathematician from the Massachusetts Institute of Technology (MIT) Peter Shor, who was working at AT&T at the time, disclosed that if a completely working quantum computer was accessible, it could factor huge numbers effectively.

In any case, I would prefer not to factor enormous numbers...

No one needs to factor enormous numbers! That is on the grounds that it's so troublesome – in any event, for the best computers on the planet today. Indeed, the trouble of calculating enormous numbers is the basis for quite a bit of our present day cryptography. It depends on math problems that are too difficult to even consider solving. RSA encryption, the technique used to encode your Visa number when you're shopping on the web, depends totally on the calculating issue. The site you need to buy from gives you an enormous "open" key (which anybody can access) to encode your charge card data.

This key really is the result of two exceptionally enormous prime numbers, known uniquely to the vender. The main way anybody could catch your data is to know those two prime numbers that increase to make the key. Since figuring is exceptionally hard, no meddler will have the option to get to your Visa number and your ledger is protected. Except if, that is, someone has manufactured a quantum computer and is running Peter Shor's calculation!

Pause... so a quantum computer will have the option to hack into my private information? That is bad.

Try not to stress classical cryptography is not totally imperiled. Albeit certain parts of classical cryptography would be endangered by quantum computing, quantum mechanics additionally takes into account another kind of profoundly secure cryptography.

How about we take a gander at a typical cryptographic convention called the one-time cushion: Say party An and party B (how about we call them Alice and Bob) share a long string of arbitrary zeros and ones — the mystery key. For whatever length of time that they just utilize this key once and they are the main ones who know this key, they can transmit a mystery message with the end goal that no meddler (we'll call her Eve) will have the option to interpret the message. The primary trouble with the one-time cushion is the real distribution of the mystery key. Before, governments sent individuals to trade books loaded with irregular information to be utilized as keys. That, obviously, is unrealistic and flawed. This is the place quantum mechanics comes in convenient by and by: Quantum Key Distribution (QKD) considers the distribution of totally arbitrary keys a ways off.

In what manner can quantum mechanics make these ultra-mystery keys?

Quantum key distribution depends on another fascinating property of quantum mechanics: any endeavor to watch or gauge a quantum framework will disturb it.

The Institute for Quantum Computing (IQC) is home of one of only a handful few QKD models on the planet. "Alice," a gadget situated at IQC home office, gets half of the trapped (exceptionally associated) photon pair produced by a laser on the top of a structure at the University of Waterloo. "Bounce" is housed at the close by Perimeter Institute, and gets the other portion of the ensnared photons.

Photons have a special quantifiable property called polarization (which should sound recognizable to any connoisseur of shades).

Since the polarization of every individual photon is arbitrary, it is highly unlikely of knowing the special properties of every photon ahead of time. In any case, here is the place entrapment gets intriguing: if Alice and Bob measure the polarization of the trapped photons they get, their outcomes will be the equivalent (recollect, "entrapped" signifies the particles are exceptionally corresponded with one another, even at significant stretches). Contingent upon the polarization of every photon, Alice and Bob attribute either a "one" or a "zero" to every photon they get. In this manner, if Alice gets a string like 010110, Bob additionally gets a 010110. Except if, that is, a busybody has been endeavoring to keep an eye on the sign.

This will disturb the framework, and Alice and Bob will in a flash notification that their keys don't coordinate.

Alice and Bob continue getting photons until their keys are long and indistinguishable enough and, voila, they have ultra-secure keys for encoding correspondences.

So tackling the quantum world can break and make codes. Something else?

Bounty. For instance, quantum computers will have the option to productively recreate quantum frameworks, which is the thing that well known physicist Richard Feynman proposed in 1982, successfully launching the field. Reenactment of quantum frameworks has been said to be a "sacred goal" of quantum computing: it will permit us to consider, in astounding point of interest, the communications among iotas and particles. This could assist us with planning new medications and new materials, for example, superconductors that work at room temperature. One more of the numerous undertakings for which the quantum computer is inalienably quicker than a classical computer is at looking through a space of potential answers for the best arrangement. Researchers are continually taking a shot at new quantum algorithms and applications. However, the genuine capability of quantum computers likely hasn't been envisioned at this point. The innovators of the laser without a doubt didn't envision grocery store checkout scanners, CD players and eye medical procedure. Also, the future employments of quantum computers are bound uniquely by creative mind.

Sounds extraordinary! Where would i be able to get a quantum computer?

One moment. While quantum computers have been hypothetically exhibited to have staggering potential, and scientists are working at IQC and around the globe to understand that potential, there is a lot of work to be done before quantum computers hit the market.

What is required to assemble a quantum computer?

Basically: we need qubits that act the manner in which we need them to. These qubits could be made of photons, iotas, electrons, particles or maybe something different. Scientists at IQC are researching an enormous cluster of them as potential bases for quantum computers. Be that as it may, qubits are famously precarious to control, since any disturbance makes them drop out of their quantum state (or "decohere"). Decoherence is the Achilles impact point of quantum computing, however it is not unfavorable. The field of quantum mistake amendment inspects how to fight off decoherence and battle different blunders. Consistently, researchers at IQC and around the globe are discovering better approaches to make qubits participate.

So when will there be a genuine quantum computer?

It relies upon your definition. There are quantum computers as of now, yet not of adequate capacity to supplant classical computers. A group of researchers from IQC and MIT hold the ebb and flow world record for the most number of qubits utilized in a trial (12). While down to earth quantum advances are as of now rising — including profoundly viable sensors, actuators and different gadgets — a genuine quantum computer that beats a classical computer is still years away. Theorists are ceaselessly making sense of better approaches to defeat decoherence, while experimentalists are increasing increasingly more authority over the quantum world through different advances and instruments. The spearheading work being done today is making ready for the coming quantum period.

So quantum technology is still years away?

No, quantum innovations are as of now being used! QKD is now financially accessible, and will incredibly profit by new research (scientists at IQC are as of now seeking after quantum encryption through free space by means of satellite). Albeit a completely working quantum computer is a more drawn out term objective, numerous major and commonsense discoveries have been made for the sake of quantum computing. Quantum sensors and actuators will permit scientists to explore the nano-scale world with astounding precision and affectability. Such devices will be significant to the advancement of genuine quantum data processors.

The quantum upheaval is now under way, and the conceivable outcomes that lie ahead are boundless.

Are Quantum Computers a Reality or Just a Scientists Dream?

Are Quantum Computers a Reality or Just a Scientists Wet Dream? The short response to that question is, yes! Quantum Computers are a reality, yet just not down to earth yet.

Have you seen the film Iron Man and his talking, thinking computer or Terminator, the robot with a spirit yet? Shouldn't something be said about a book that portrays an anecdotal innovation that far surpasses our present degree of information?

In the event that you have, at that point you would be directly in imagining that the present handling paces of our quickest computers won't approach what you have seen. You may contend that with enough computational force we could make copycat insight, (This is my favored depiction of man-made consciousness as I accept, we will never make computerized reasoning that thinks, feels and is mindful of itself. Scientists will persuade this is conceivable that by one way or another on the off chance that you gather enough preparing force into one gadget it will inevitably simply like enchantment become mindful of itself).

Anyway, you would never fabricate a handy gadget that could test a boundless measure of handling power. as it would without a doubt glitch on many occasions, because of keeping such a gadget cool and kept up sufficiently long to quantify such properties, and indeed, even with the present size of processors breaking records for size decrease, you would in any case need a ton of them to give the investigation a run for its cash.

Quantum Processors offer expectation and they are coming our direction sooner, instead of later, not as I have said for computers with a spirit, that is the obligation of a more noteworthy and random science, however for computational gadgets that have boundless preparing power and will never experience the ill effects of delayed down with graphical applications like gaming consoles, or need time to render information from a detonating star.

In June of 2009 a group of scientists from the Yale University made a Solid State Quantum Processor! A processor that uses the laws of Quantum Physics to figure, rather than 0's and 1's. The processor has just exhibited that it is conceivable to make such a gadget, yet is still in its beginning times and has no down to earth use. Anyway, it answers the title of this article with a YES!

I won't attempt to clarify Quantum Physics in this article, it would be better in the event that you read a book regarding the matter, it would be ideal if you remark on this article, my speculation is you would think that its befuddling. I will be that as it may, clarify the significant distinction between a Quantum Processor and a lowland standard dependable Intel Processor.

The Intel Processor will register an issue with 1's and 0's which implies On, Off. Solids state the Intel Processor needs to glance through a variety of Social Security Numbers, after you input your very own Social Security Number for a match.

The Intel Processor will go down the list individually, until it either finds a match or arrives at the finish of the list. This is tedious and bigger lists will begin to show the cutoff points of the processor.

Presently the Quantum Processor has an incredible favorable position over a standard Processor like the one above. In view of the Laws of Quantum Physics the Quantum Processor can check the entire list as though it was just checking only one Social Security Number. At the end of the day the Quantum Processor, can figure with no genuine breaking points to its speed.

A Quantum Processor would set aside a similar effort to figure a list of 100,000 Social Security numbers as it would take to register a list of only one Social Security number!

Why Quantum Computing?

Quantum Mechanics (QM) portrays the conduct and properties of rudimentary particles, for example, electrons or photons on the nuclear and subatomic levels. Defined in the primary portion of the twentieth century basically by Schrodinger [Sch26], Bohr [Boh08], Heisenberg [Cas] and Dirac [Dir95], it was uniquely in the late 70's that quantum data handling frameworks has been proposed [Pop75, Ing76, Man80]. Considerably later, in the 80's of the only remaining centuries it was Feynman who proposed the primary physical acknowledgment of a Quantum Computer [Fey85]. In corresponding to Feynman, Benioff [Ben82] likewise was one of the main researchers to figure the standards of quantum computing and Deutsch proposed the principal Quantum Algorithm [Deu85]. The explanation that these ideas are happening to enthusiasm to computer designing network is fundamentally because of the Moore's law [Moo65]; that is: the quantity of transistors in a chip pairs like clockwork and the size of entryways is continually contracting. Thus problems, for example, heat dissipation and data misfortune are getting significant for present and future advances. Improving the size of transistors eventually prompts a technology taking a shot at the degree of rudimentary particles, for example, a solitary electron or photon. Since Moore's paper the advancement prompted the current 35 nm (3.5 * 10−10m) circuit technology which thinking about the size of an iota (roughly 10−10m) is generally near the nuclear size. Thus, the investigation of QM and its related Quantum Computing turns out to be very important to the advancement of logic structure of future gadgets and in outcome to the improvement of quantum algorithms, quantum CAD and quantum logic synthesis and engineering systems and speculations. On account of their prevalent exhibition and explicit issue related properties, quantum computers will be transcendently utilized in computational insight and mechanical technology, and comparatively to old style computers they will at last enter each region of technology and everyday life.

Regardless of the reality of being founded on dumbfounding standards, QM has discovered applications in practically all fields of logical research and technology. However, the most significant hypothetical and in the future additionally pragmatic developments were done in the field of Quantum computing, quantum data, and quantum circuits structure [BBC+ 95, SD96].

Albeit just hypothetical ideas of usage of complete quantum computer designs have been proposed [BBC+ 95, Fey85, Ben82, Deu85] the continuous advances in technology will permit the development of Quantum Computers in close future, maybe in the interim of 10 to 50 years. Ongoing advancement in usage and designs prove that this territory is exactly at its beginning and is growing. For example, the execution of little quantum logic show tons with caught molecules or particles [BBC+95, NC00, CZ95, DKK03, PW02] are the sign that this time allotment of close future can be conceivably decreased to just a couple of years before the first completely quantum computer is developed. The biggest forward-thinking usage of quantum computer is the adiabatic computer by DWAVE [AOR+ 02, AS04, vdPIG+ 06, ALT08, HJL+10]. In spite of the fact that up to now it is as yet an open issue whether the DWAVE computer is an appropriate quantum computer or not [], it gives considerable accelerate over old style computer in the SAT execution and int the Random Number Generation []. In corresponding to the adiabatic quantum computer, models for full quantum computers have been proposed [MOC02, SO02, MC]. In these propositions the quantum calculations is actualized over a lot of flying-photons that speaks to the level of opportunity of associations between qubits. Such models anyway have not been executed starting at yet.

This part displays the essential ideas of quantum computing just as the transition from quantum material science to quantum computing. We likewise present quantum computing models, important to comprehend our ideas of quantum logic, quantum computing and synthesis of quantum logic circuits.

How Quantum Computers Will Work

Quantum computers open up another period for fast calculations. They will be multiple times quicker than current silicon-based computers. The present fast computer sitting before you is essentially the same as its 30-ton predecessors, which were outfitted with nearly 18,000 vacuum tubes and 805 kilometers (500 miles) of wiring!

Moore's law:

In 1965, Intel prime supporter Gordon Moore saw what's to come. His forecast, prevalently known as Moore's Law, expresses that the quantity of transistors on a chip pairs about at regular intervals. This perception about silicon mix, made a reality by Intel, has powered the overall technology transformation.

In a quantum computer, the basic unit of data (called a quantum bit or qubit), is not paired but instead progressively quaternary in nature. This qubit property arises as an immediate outcome of its adherence to the laws of quantum mechanics which contrast fundamentally from the laws of old style material science. A qubit can exist not just in a state comparing to the coherent state 0 or 1 as in a traditional piece, yet in addition in states relating to a mix or superposition of these old style states.

The intensity of quantum

Computers:

As the technology advances, a few components cooperate to push us toward quantum computing, and push out the old style silicon-based chips. These elements are scaling in size, vitality utilization, financial aspects of building driving At the present pace of chip scaling down, vitality proficiency and financial matters, the traditional computer of the year 2020 (on the off chance that it could occur by any means) would contain a CPU running at 40 GHz (or 40,000 MHz), with 160 GB (160,000 MB) of arbitrary access memory (RAM), and run on 40 watts of intensity.

Scaling: The computing scene is loaded with advancements, and huge numbers of them include all the more dominant and littler chips. Chip limit has multiplied each year and a half, as indicated by Moore's Law, however, the chip size stays steady. The number of transistors on a solitary chip is additionally rising exponentially. It appears that in the event that scaling down proceeds at the current rate, a piece will be spoken to by a single particle constantly 2020.

Future Computers:

Particles Packed In An "Egg Carton" Of Light?

Scientists at Ohio State University have stepped toward the advancement of amazing new computers - by making minor gaps that contain nothing by any stretch of the imagination.

The openings - dim spots in an egg container molded surface of laser light - would one be able to day support molecules for quantum computing

Central confinement to quantum computers

Quantum computers that store data in purported quantum bits (or qubits) will be stood up to with a major impediment. This is the case made by Dutch hypothetical physicists from the Foundation for Fundamental Research on Matter (FOM).

Obstructions and Research:

The researchers said that the potential for quantum computing is tremendous, and that ongoing advancement has been empowering - however there are as yet numerous deterrents to defeat before quantum computers become financially accessible. To be practical, quantum computers must have in any event a few dozen qubits before they will be able to solve true problems.

At present, research is in progress to discover techniques for doing combating the dangerous impacts of decoherence to build up an ideal equipment engineering for planning and building a quantum computer, and to additionally reveal quantum algorithms to use the gigantic computing power accessible in these gadgets. Normally this interest is personally identified with quantum blunder remedy codes and quantum algorithms.

The Future Is Quantum

Quantum resembles an extension between what's conceivable and what's likely. It makes sci-fi science truth, and it's here. All things considered, practically here. The issue of quantum computing has been baffling researchers for about 3 decades, and now it would seem that we're just a couple of brief years from getting them from our nearby tech stores.

What's the serious deal with quantum computers at any rate? All things considered, they're super-quick and super-effective, making current PCs resemble the gigantic machines that occupied a whole space when they were first created. As per Fred Chong, from the University to California, a quantum computer would have the option to solve in unimportant months problems that would take a traditional computer a large number of years.

The way in to their "superness" is the way that quantum bits or qubits are not bound by the shows of reality as we probably am aware them. Typical electrons turn either clockwise or against clockwise. Quantum electrons turn in the two headings without a moment's delay. This capacity to rise above a solitary reality implies that when they're utilized in computing, quantum electrons change regular "bits" into qubits. Regular bits can be either a 1 or a 0, however qubits can be both simultaneously.

In quantum mechanical terms, the qubits exist in superposition, which prompts an inborn parallelism, which as indicated by physicist David Deutsch permits quantum computers to take a shot at a million calculations without a moment's delay. Current PCs can chip away at just one.

One of the most significant advantages of quantum computers, beside the various "superness", is that they'll make silicon based microchips out of date. This is something worth being thankful for in light of the fact that inside around 4 years silicon chips will have advanced themselves out of existence, being too little to even think about being of any viable use.

One of the manners by which they'll discredit silicon chips, and totally upset the manner in which computers are wired, is through the quantum property of teleportation. Utilizing teleportation, data around one molecule will be transmitted to another without utilizing any wires whatsoever. In Star Trek terms, data is shot starting with one molecule then onto the next. The pleasant thing about quantum is that there will consistently be sufficient capacity to do this. No thrashing about in space, freezing about another Klingon assault for these infants. You're in every case great to go.

Straightforward quantum computers are as of now in existence, however they're not even close to accomplishing what they're able to do. In 2007, a Canadian organization, D-Wave, made a 16-qubit (the objective is at any rate 30 qubits) quantum computer that could solve sudoku bewilders. Other quantum computers can solve the question of Schrodinger's feline (a feline in a container with poison, is it alive or dead? Until you open the container and see, it possesses the two states, similar to quantum electrons and qubits), thought about one of the most significant conditions in quantum mechanics.

Quantum Mechanics To Interpret Or Not To Interpret

Quantum theory is, as a matter of first importance, a profoundly progressed numerical apparatus that works.

The science of this progressive theory advanced out of a pragmatic need to control explicit scientific gear and to convey data about explicit test systems. As the best scientific theory ever, quantum theory needs no ontological understanding. Its most prepared professionals, indeed, don't perceive ontological cases as legitimate cases.

Philosophical Differences

Cosmology is the investigation of what is. Epistemology is the investigation of what we can know.

Metaphysics works on the key premise that there is an existence as of now set up to discover. Epistemology, by comparison, questions any existence at all, until we can watch it in precise terms. Quantum theory, in this manner, is the embodiment of epistemology, since physicists who apply it most for all intents and purposes permit a bad situation for ontological suspicions about genuine articles that exist preceding perceptions and estimations.

In the standard way wherein numerous physicists use quantum theory, perceptions and estimations are the main substantial roads to real information. Anything that we can't watch and gauge in quantum terms, along these lines, has no reality. On the off chance that we watch just probabilities of watching given occasions, at that point the most we can say about the truth is as far as those probabilities. Any extra hypotheses are fictions.

The State Of Reality

The cutting edge scientific thought of "the truth" is on exceptionally unstable grounds, since present day scientific theories have wandered a long way from human detects that have constantly offered importance to our clearly physical world. A few people may state that the present thought of "the truth" is in a sorry state. Quantum physicists, obviously, would state this is an unscientific judgment and concede to their precisely characterized scientific "state vector" as the main conceivable depiction of the real world.

Such dedication to numerical strategy appears to be chilling to individuals conventionally familiar with increasingly inventive viewpoints. Scientific precision, be that as it may, permits just for numerical creative mind, which is just as wild as some other inventive thinker's, however just in those specialists who have aced math's different structures. Then again, numerical creative mind is not as open as artistic creative mind, and this, I accept, is the wellspring of most contentions about how to decipher quantum math. A significant number of the individuals contending over understandings essentially are not prepared in math, yet these individuals look for a non-scientific reverberation with numerical scholars, in any case, and I propose this is a sensible objective.

The Real Argument

I may even surrender that there can be no authentic scientific contention about the "best translation" of quantum theory, and by "understanding," I signify "ontological translation." Clearly, the theory takes into account an assortment of ontological understandings. Contentions about ontological understandings, at that point, are stylish contentions, and tasteful contentions have legitimacy in their very own areas (i.e., expressions of the human experience).

For what reason are there such warmed contentions about a "best translation" of quantum mechanics?

The response to this inquiry is that people by and large need more than precise apparatuses to assemble a significant life. We need a sentimental vision to envelop our precisely estimated perceptions. We need a more extensive standpoint to encase our anatomical and physiological structures. We need a calculated interface between tactile discernments and hypothetical strategies. Such an interface is without a doubt tasteful, as we people locate our most noteworthy inspirations in an item's or a thought's stylish intrigue.

Indeed, even science can suit feel to speak to the more noteworthy culture in which it is installed. Scientific theories, in this manner, can't get away from the destiny of being chic or out of style.

The Adiabatic Quantum Computing Model

The adiabatic quantum computing model was proposed in 2000 by Farhi et al. [145] who recommended a calculation to solve advancement problems, for example, SATISFIABILITY (SAT); there is present proof that this calculation sets aside an exponential effort for a few (nondeterministic polynomial time) NP-complete problems. The enthusiasm for the adiabatic quantum computing was recharged in 2005 when Aharonov et al. demonstrated that it is identical to the quantum circuit model.

An adiabatic procedure is a semi-static thermodynamic process when no warmth is moved; something contrary to an adiabatic system is an isothermal procedure when the heat is transferred to keep up the temperature consistent. An adiabatic advancement of a quantum framework implies that the Hamiltonian is gradually changing; review from Section 1.6 that the Hamiltonian administrator compares to the absolute vitality of the quantum framework. The Hamiltonian is a Hermitian administrator, and its eigenvector comparing to the littlest eigenvalue (i.e., to the most minimal complete dynamism of the frame) is known as the ground condition of the framework. A neighborhood Hamiltonian depicts a quantum framework where the connections happen just among a consistent and rather little, number of particles.

The adiabatic estimation is a standard strategy to infer surmised answers for the Schrödinger condition when the Hamiltonian is gradually fluctuating. This strategy depends on an honest thought: If the quantum framework is set up in a ground state and the Hamiltonian differs slowly enough, at that point, over the long haul, the structure will remain in a country near to the ground condition of the immediate Hamiltonian. This thought is caught by the adiabatic hypothesis of Born and Fock.

A solid framework stays in its immediate eigenstate if a given bother is following up on it gradually enough and if there is a hole between the eigenvalues (comparing to this eigenstate) and the remainder of the Hamiltonian's range.

Consider a quantum framework in the state $|\psi(t)\rangle$, Hn, with a Hamiltonian, H(t). The Schrödinger condition depicts the development of the framework,

$$i\frac{d}{dt}|\psi(t)\rangle = H(t)|\psi(t)\rangle$$

Accept that the Hamiltonian H(t) is gradually changing:

$$H(t) = \tilde{H}(t/T),$$

where T controls the pace of variety of H(t), and $\tilde{H}(t/T)$ has a place with a smooth one-parameter group of Hamiltonians, $\tilde{H}(s)$, $0 \leq s \leq 1$. The immediate eigenstates, $|i;s\rangle$, and eigenvalues, E_i, of $\tilde{H}(s)$ are characterized as

$$\tilde{H}(s)|i;s\rangle = E_i|i;s\rangle$$

The eigenvalues of $\tilde{H}(s)$ are requested.

$E0(s) \leq E1(s) \leq \ldots \leq En(s)$

Calls $|\psi 0\rangle = |\ |\ = |i=0; s=0\rangle$ the ground territory of $\tilde{H}(0)$. The adiabatic hypothesis says that if the hole between the most minimal vitality levels $E1(s) - E0(s) < 0, \forall\ 0 \leq s \leq 1$, at that point the state, $|\psi(t)\rangle$, of the framework after an advancement portrayed by the Schrödinger condition, will be near the ground condition of this Hamiltonian $H(t)$ for $0 \leq t \leq T$ when T is sufficiently huge.

The adiabatic quantum computer advances between an underlying state with the Hamiltonian, Hint, and the last state with the Hamiltonian, Final. The info information and the calculation are encoded as the ground province of Hint, and the consequence of the calculation is the ground territory of Hfinal. The running time of the adiabatic computation is dictated by the insignificant otherworldly hole of all Hamiltonians of the structure

$H(s) = (1-s)Hinit + sHffina[, 0 \leq s \leq 1$

This is Hamiltonians lie on the straight line interfacing Hint and Hfinal [3]. The ground condition of the Hamiltonian Hfinal for the improvement calculation in [145] was an old-style stated in the computational basis, and Hfinal was a corner to corner lattice as the arrangement of a combinatorial enhancement issue. This limitation was evacuated by Aharonov et al., which requires just that the Hamiltonians be the neighborhood. This condition looks like the one forced on the quantum circuit model—to be specific, that the quantum doors work on a steady number of qubits.

Quantum Logic

Logic minimization is an outstanding region of computer building and in this book different new research viewpoints identified with search, robotized synthesis and minimization of quantum circuits are discussed. In Quantum Logic Synthesis, the methods utilized are straightforwardly identified with the portrayals that are being applied. For these portrayals different approaches are utilized while orchestrating FSM's, Logic Circuits, Behaviors or Quantum Cellular Automata. For example inside evolutionary approaches, to combine a FSM utilizing developmental methodology, the most noticeable strategy incorporates the Genetic Programming [Koz92, Koz94] while the synthesis of Boolean logic capacities or circuits has chiefly been finished utilizing the Genetic Algorithm. Algorithmic techniques, for example, structure or otherworldly synthesis [SBM05a,SBM05b,Mil02,MMD06,PARK+01,KPK02,GAJ06,FTR07,WGMD09, SZSS10, PLKK10] have been utilized also.

In this section presented are ideas of quantum logic synthesis as for quantum natives and their expenses. We portray a general technique for the synthesis of quantum circuits. Different heuristics are examined on the utilitarian level so as to show logic synthesis strategies utilized for Machine Learning (Chapter ??). The depicted ideas present the expense of quantum entryways utilized in our synthesis strategies and specifically we examine the quantum inductive inclination on the logic synthesis of circuits that can be utilized in the control of conduct robots utilizing inductive AI.

Past research on robotized synthesis of quantum circuits

The quest for littler, less expensive and preferably ideal circuits in quantum and reversible logic prompted a lot of entryways and circuits usually utilized as all inclusive insignificant natives for logic synthesis [BBC+ 95, Per00, SD96, HSY+ 04]. There are a few properties that are being looked for and some of them are: comprehensiveness, low realization cost, technology particularity and great synthesis properties. By and large, the objective is an aggregate of the referenced sub-objectives with a different level of significance for each and every one of these objectives. Be that as it may, contingent upon the multifaceted nature of the characterized issue, it is likewise required to precisely determine the fractional objectives and investigate them independently.

It was appeared by [DiV95, DiV95, SD96, MML+ 98, Per00] that all doors (quantum circuits) with more than 1 qubit could be assemble utilizing only one-qubit and chose two-qubit natives. A major test is to fabricate the essential potential doors, for example, Fredkin [SD96, LPG+04] or Toffoli having the littlest expense for a given technology. As indicated by the portrayal of quantum logic in Chapter 1, unmistakably logic synthesis of quantum circuits consists in discovering structures of crude doors with the end goal that their resultant lattice is equivalent to the particular unitary network.

This issue can be found in a similarity to planning traditional logic circuits from fundamental logic doors utilizing a particular in type of a Karnaugh Map (KMap) [DM94]. As was appeared in [LPG+04] the synthesis of quantum circuits is a non-monotonic starches and therefore it is difficult to utilize robotized systems to quantum circuit synthesis without depending on certain heuristics. Additionally, as can be suggested from matrices speaking to entryways or circuits, their dimensionality develops exponentially with the quantity of qubits.

For instance, a circuit with 3 qubits will be spoken to by a grid of 23 by 23 (64 components) while a circuit with 5 qubits will have a lattice of size 25 by 25 (1024 components). Every component of such a lattice is by and large a com-plex number and therefore the count of the network may in the most pessimistic scenario request likewise an exponential time. In addition, in quantum logic synthesis all circuits can be created from numerous points of view utilizing quantum doors and without including more qubits. At the end of the day, a circuit given by a Unitary change U, can be acknowledged either from a base number of doors or can be acknowledged in limitlessly numerous circuits of different costs; the more part entryways accessible as the information set, the more answers for the synthesis are conceivable. Accordingly, the issue of minimization in Quantum Logic Synthesis is not just an issue of exponentially growing the arrangement space with the size of the circuit yet in addition that of finding the insignificant arrangement of doors that would permit a possibly negligible arrangement.

With no requirements, the synthesis issue depicted in the past passage, is NP; the way toward orchestrating a circuit with k-quantum entryways can be viewed as the issue of subset-entirety (rucksack) [GJ79, CLRS01] issue. To see this, it is sufficient to consider an underlying limited size arrangement of quantum entryways and the issue is to ask whether yes or not there is a circuit with k-doors executing capacity f? This portrayal is practically equivalent to the Knapsack issue. Specifically relying upon technology, the test is to assemble any general entryway utilizing only one-qubit and two-qubit natives.

The greater part of realized quantum circuits synthesis procedures are either for few qubits just, for few doors or for certain particular obliged logic groups of capacities, (for example, reversible or direct capacities). The most widely recognized Quantum Logic Synthesis (QLS) approaches are utilized for the plan of simply quantum permutative (reversible) logic circuits [MD03,LPG+04,LP02,YHSP05,YSPH05, MDM05, SBM05a, SBM05b, MDM07, HSY+ 06, WGMD09, PLKK10, ?]. The synthesis of the reversible circuits can be additionally part into two fundamental subcategories; one way to deal with the reversible logic configuration depends vigorously on the use of the ancilla bits [MD03,MDM05,WGMD09], the subsequent methodology structures reversible logic circuits just on the insignificant number of qubits [MP02, LPG+04, YHSP05, FTR07, ?, LSKed]. The general technique isolating these two standards of reversible logic synthesis is that countless ancilla qubits can conceivably lessen the quantity of the necessary entryways to integrate a circuit at a cost of the ancilla bits [MWD10].

An increasingly broad QLS for discretionary quantum circuits was performed from a lot more modest number of qubits [Yab00, Rub01, LPG+03, LSKed]. This methodology was all in all progressively test up to now because of the way that there is possibly an unending number of quantum entryways that can be utilized for the QLS. In these methodologies a solitary calculation - a hereditary calculation - was utilized to structure or upgraded a quantum circuit.

Consequently,in spite of some previously revealed outcomes from the QLS approach there is no broad technique to orchestrate bigger than 2-qubit quantum circuits utilizing quantum non permutative natives. A portion of the techniques are adjusted from Reversible logic synthesis and have been utilized essentially for synthesis utilizing the CNT set of entryways (NOT, Feynman and Toffoli) or comparative libraries not permitting to utilize the whole force offered by the quantum circuits and quantum logic. There exists additionally a little arrangement of different new libraries of doors for quantum logic synthesis [BBC+ 95, SD96, LP02, YSPH05, LPK10].

Among these methodologies likewise exists techniques utilizing the supposed Multi-Controlled Toffoli (MCT) entryways as the one of a kind synthesis part door [MMD03, MDM05, MDM07, WGMD09, PLKK10] where the capacity structured as a circuit is solely based from the Toffoli doors. Closer to the quantum equipment usage is for example the methodology proposed in [SBM05a] where the synthesis of the reversible doors is finished utilizing the purported quantum multiplexer. Anyway, there is no confirmation that any of them has the negligible quantum acknowledgment cost regarding all circuits that can be work for the given useful determination. Along these lines it is as yet an open issue to discover which set of entryways will permit to produce a least exorbitant circuit (in the quantity of doors and in the quantity of ancilla bits) for different innovations.

Quantum Advantage

The Quantum Advantage achievement accept explicit quantum calculation benchmarks43 that would resist reproduction on classical computers. Google has as of late proposed such benchmarks for a specific examining issue, prodding genuine upgrades in reenactment algorithms.

As a symptom, researchers found various escape clauses in the benchmarks that make reproduction a lot simpler. Realized escape clauses have been shut at the point when Google published revised benchmarks.

When all is said in done, we anticipate there will be a time of feline and-mouse as escape clauses rise and are shut again in quantum advantage benchmarks.

As one model, groupings of corner to corner doors ought to be maintained a strategic distance from on the grounds that they empower effective tensor-organize compression strategies.

Computational-basis estimations applied after corner to corner entryways can likewise be misused.

Now and again, these and different escape clauses have properties that can be checked by confirmation strategies.

Scientists Hint at Smartphone – Sized Quantum Computers

Researchers state cell phone measured quantum computers could be created with the assistance of microwaves and particles, alluding to the plausibility of littler quantum computing gadgets in the future.

Physicists at the National Institute of Standards and Technology (NIST) have just because connected the quantum properties of two isolated particles by controlling them with microwaves as opposed to the typical laser bars.

They propose it might be conceivable to supplant a colorful room-sized quantum computing "laser park" with scaled-down, business microwave technology like that utilized in advanced cells.

"It's possible an unobtrusive estimated quantum computer could inevitably seem as though an advanced mobile phone joined with a laser pointer-like gadget, while sophisticated machines may have a general impression practically identical to a standard work area PC," says NIST physicist Dietrich Leibfried.

Scientists state microwave parts could be extended and overhauled all the more effectually to construct down to earth frameworks of thousands of particles for quantum computing and reproductions, contrasted with perplexing, costly laser sources.

Even though microwaves, the bearer of remote correspondences, have been utilized before control single particles, NIST researchers are the first to situate microwaves sources sufficiently close to the particles only 30 micrometers away-and make the conditions empowering ensnarement.

The snare is a quantum wonder expected to be critical for shipping data and redressing blunders in quantum computers.

Scientists incorporated wiring for microwave sources straightforwardly on a chip-sized particle trap and utilized a work area scale table of lasers, mirrors, and focal points that is just around one-tenth of the size recently required. Even though low-power bright lasers are as yet expected to cool the particles and watch exploratory outcomes, it may, in the long run, be made as little as those in versatile DVD players.

"Even though quantum computers are not thought of as comfort gadgets that everyone needs to haul around, they could utilize microwave hardware like what is utilized in PDAs. These parts are very much produced for a mass-market to help advancement and diminish costs. The possibility energizes us," Leibfried included.

Particles are a primary possibility for use as quantum bits, or qubits, to hold data in a quantum computer. Albeit another promising contender for qubits-outstandingly superconducting circuits, or "counterfeit molecules"- are controlled on chips with microwaves, particle qubits are at a further developed stage tentatively in that more particles can be controlled with better exactness and less loss of data.

In the most recent trials, the NIST group utilized microwaves to pivot the "turns" of individual magnesium particles and snare the twists of a couple of particles. This is an "all-inclusive" arrangement of quantum logic activities since revolutions and snare can be consolidated in succession to play out any computation permitted by quantum mechanics, Leibfried says.

In the tests, the two particles were held by electromagnetic fields, drifting over a particle trap chip consisting of gold terminals electroplated onto an aluminum nitride backing. A portion of the anodes was actuated to make beats of wavering microwave radiation around the particles. Radiations frequencies are in the 1 to 2 gigahertz extend.

The microwaves produce attractive fields used to pivot the particles' twists, which can be thought of as small bar magnets pointing in various ways. The direction of these small bar magnets is one of the quantum properties used to speak to data.

Scientists trapped the particles by adjusting a procedure they created with lasers. On the off chance that the microwaves' attractive fields step by step increment over the particles in the perfect way, the particles' movement can be energized, relying upon the turn directions, and the twists can get caught all the while.

Scientists needed to locate the correct blend of settings in the three cathodes that gave the ideal change in the swaying attractive fields over the degree of the particles' movement while limiting other, undesirable impacts. The properties of the snared particles are connected, with the end goal that an estimation of one particle would uncover the condition of the other.

A quantum computer is a gadget for calculation utilizing quantum mechanical wonders, for example, superposition and snare, to perform activities on the information. The essential rule behind the quantum calculation is that quantum properties can be utilized to speak to report and perform operations on this information.

Quantum computers would saddle the strange guidelines of quantum material science to solve specific problems, for example, breaking the existing most generally utilized information encryption codes, which areas of now obstinate even with supercomputers.

A closer term objective is to plan quantum reproductions of significant scientific problems, to investigate quantum puzzles, for example, high-temperature superconductivity, the disappearance of electrical resistance in specific materials when adequately chilled.

Scientists state the utilization of microwaves decreases blunders presented by insecurities in laser shaft pointing and power just as laser-instigated unconstrained emissions by the particles. Be that as it may, microwave tasks should be improved to empower functional quantum calculations or reproductions.

Is Quantum Computing Closer Than We Thought?

Quantum computing could prepare for better computer equipment technology in the anticipating future. Let's be honest - 'its an obvious fact that silicon is arriving at its impediments for use in microprocessors', so what sort of advancements would we be able to hope to rise, and would they say they are nearer than we suspected?

The most discussed point you will catch wind of as respects to future processors and technological movement is 'quantum computing'. Right now - current processors utilize twofold code consisting of 1's and 0's to adhere to guidelines, encode, interpret and perform counts. However, quantum technology will revolutionize current technology as the theory of quantum computing, is to control the turn of electrons (quantum particles), in this way an electron can move in both of two bearings, just as having vague turn positions, known as quantum states. This permits an electron to speak to either '1' or '0' simultaneously, which is the basis for the possibly tremendous force a quantum computer could give.

Besides - When a quantum processor stores this data - it does as such in 'qubits', incredibly - it would then be able to mastermind these all the while to gain each conceivable result. The force a quantum processor could give would be useful to computers, however perhaps would extraordinarily assist us with making future scientific and therapeutic advances more than ever? as present silicon based processors come up short on the force, proficiency and exactness to compute the multifaceted nature of particles.

Qubits and Quantum Memory

In old style calculation, the unit of data is a piece, which can be 0 or 1. In quantum computation, this unit is a quantum bit (qubit), which is a superposition of 0 and 1. Consider a framework with 2 basis states, call them j0i and j1i. We distinguish these basis states with the two symmetrical vectors 1 and 0, separately. A solitary qubit can be in any superposition

0   1

0j0i + 1j1i; j 0j2 + j 1j2 = 1:

In like manner, a solitary qubit \lives" in the vector space C2.

Additionally, we can consider frameworks of more than 1 qubit, which \live" in the tensor item space of a few qubit frameworks. For example, a 2-qubit framework has 4 basis states: j0i, j0i j1i, j1i j0i, j1i. Here for example j1i j0i implies that the rst qubit is in its basis state j1i and the second qubit is in its basis state j0i. We will regularly curtail this to j1ij0i, j1; 0i, or even j10i.

All the more for the most part, a register of n qubits has 2n basis expresses, every one of the structure jb1 I jb2i :jbni, with bi 2 f0; 1g. We can abridge this to jb1b2 :bni. We will frequently curtail 0 : 0 to 0n. Since bitstrings of length n can be seen as whole numbers somewhere in the range of 0 and 2n 1 (see Appendix B.2), we can likewise compose the basis states as numbers j0i; j1i; j2i; : ; j2n 1i. Note that the vector comparing to n-qubit basis state jxi is the 2n-dimensional vector that has a 1 at the x-th position and 0s somewhere else (here we see x as a whole number in $\{0, \ldots, 2^n-1\}$ and we include the situations in the vector beginning from position 0). This suggests two n-qubit basis states $|x\rangle$ and $|y\rangle$ are symmetrical $|x \neq y$. A different approach to see this symmetry is to utilize the standards of tensor item (Appendix A.6):

$$\langle x|y\rangle = \langle x_1|y_1\rangle \cdots \langle x_n|y_n\rangle = \langle x_1|y_1\rangle \cdots \langle x_n|y_n\rangle.$$

Since $\langle x_k|y_k\rangle = \delta_{x_k, y_k}$, we see that basis states $|x\rangle$ and $|y\rangle$ will be symmetrical when there is in any event one position k at which the bits of x and y differ.

A quantum register of n qubits can be in any superposition

$$\sum_{j=0}^{2^n-1} \alpha_j |j\rangle = \alpha_0 |0\rangle + \alpha_1 |1\rangle + \cdots + \alpha_{2^n-1} |2^n-1\rangle; \quad \sum_j |\alpha_j|^2 = 1.$$

Estimating this in the computational basis, we get the n-bit state $|j\rangle$ with likelihood $|\alpha_j|^2$. Estimating only the first qubit of a state would compare to the projective estimation that has the two projectors $P_0 = |0\rangle\langle 0| \otimes I_{2^{n-1}}$ and $P_1 = |1\rangle\langle 1| \otimes I_{2^{n-1}}$. For instance, applying this estimation to the state $\sqrt{\frac{1}{3}} |0\rangle |i\rangle + \sqrt{\frac{2}{3}} |1\rangle |j\rangle$ gives result 0 with likelihood 1/3; the state at that point becomes $|0\rangle_i$ I. We get result 1 with likelihood 2/3; the state at that point becomes $|1\rangle_i$ I. So also, estimating the first n qubits of a (n + m)- qubit state in the computational basis compares to the projective estimation that has 2^n projectors $P_j = |j\rangle\langle j| I_{2^m}$ for $j \in \{0, 1\}^n$.

A significant property that has the right to be referenced is entrapment, which alludes to quantum relationships between's different qubits. For example, consider a 2-qubit register that is in the state

$$\frac{1}{\sqrt{2}}|00\rangle + \frac{1}{\sqrt{2}}|11\rangle.$$

Such 2-qubit states are some of the time called EPR-combines out of appreciation for Einstein, Podolsky, and Rosen, who inspected such states and their apparently confusing properties. At first neither one nor the other qubits has an old style esteem $|0\rangle$ or $|1\rangle$. In any case, on the off chance that we measure the first qubit and watch, say, a $|0\rangle$, at that point the entire state crumples to $|00\rangle$. Subsequently watching the first qubit quickly fixes likewise the second, surreptitiously qubit to an old style esteem. Since the two qubits that make up the register might be far separated, this model delineates a portion of the non-nearby effects that quantum frameworks can display. As a rule, a bipartite state $|\psi\rangle$ is called snared in the event that it can't be composed as a tensor item $|A\rangle |B\rangle$ where $|A\rangle$ lives in the first space and $|B\rangle$ lives in the second.

Now, a comparison with old style likelihood distributions might be useful. Assume we have two likelihood spaces, An and B, the rst with 2n potential results, the second with 2m potential results. A likelihood distribution on the rst space can be depicted by 2n numbers (non-negative reals adding to 1; really there are just 2n 1 degrees of opportunity here) and a distribution on the second by 2m numbers. Appropriately, an item distribution on the joint space can be portrayed by 2n + 2m numbers. Be that as it may, a self-assertive (non-item) distribution on the joint space takes 2n+m genuine numbers, since there are 2n+m potential results altogether. Similarly, a n-qubit state j Ai can be portrayed by 2n numbers (complex numbers whose squared moduli aggregate to 1), a m-qubit state j Bi by 2m numbers, and their tensor item j Ai j Bi by 2n + 2m numbers. Notwithstanding, a self-assertive (conceivably snared) state in the joint space takes 2n+m numbers, since it lives in a 2n+m-dimensional space. We see that the quantity of parameters required to depict quantum states is equivalent to the quantity of parameters expected to portray likelihood distributions.

Additionally, note the relationship between statistical independence[3] of two irregular factors An and B and non-trap of the item state j Ai j Bi. Be that as it may, regardless of the similitudes among probabilities and amplitudes, quantum states are substantially more dominant than distributions, since amplitudes may have negative (or even intricate) parts which can prompt obstruction e ects. Amplitudes possibly become probabilities when we square them. The craft of quantum computing is to utilize these uncommon properties for fascinating computational purposes.

Another Hardware Alternative for ML and AI: Quantum Computing

Quantum computing is proceeding to scale up and with the ongoing declaration from the Vancouver based quantum computing organization, D-Wave, of their 2,000-qubit processor it doesn't give indications of easing back down.

D-Wave is the main quantum computing organization that has made the technology accessible for business use. The quantum computing processors are in direct challenge with the more custom kinds of chips utilized for Machine Learning and AI like GPUs and the recently declared second-age TPU from Google.

The significant piece of quantum computing is that it replaces the conventional perspective of computing. By supplanting the regular piece, 0 or 1, with another kind of data, it opens up to exponential measures of potential outcomes. The qubit can be in the superposition state where it is neither +1 or - 1 yet, it could be said it is both, and it is this that takes into account the superfast computing.

The D-Wave quantum computers utilize the way toward toughening. This includes a progression of minuscule magnets to be orchestrate on a matrix. Each attractive field impacts one another and afterward they arrange themselves into a situation to limit the measure of vitality put away in the whole field. It is during this procedure, that one can change the quality of the attractive field from every magnet with the goal that the magnets situate themselves in a manner to solve explicit problems. To find a good pace, you start with high measures of vitality so it is simple for the magnets to flip to and fro. At that point as you bring down the temperature, the magnets arrive at lower and lower levels of vitality until they are solidified into the most minimal vitality state. Here it is conceivable to peruse the direction of every magnet and discover the response to the issue. One can say that D-Wave's quantum computer is a sort of simple computer depending on Nature's algorithms to discover the design of the most reduced vitality state.

This is the place we luck out. This particular class of quantum computing happens to be helpful for a subset of streamlining computing problems, particularly those outfitted towards Machine Learning. Many Machine Learning problems can be reformulated as vitality problems. The D-Wave quantum computers are intended to help problems that need elevated level thinking followed by decision making. The quantum computing considers Artificial Intelligence or AI frameworks to mimic human manners of thinking considerably more intently than an old style processor. And keeping in mind that the possibility of quantum computing can be difficult to comprehend, its utilization in Machine Learning advance technology is unmistakably opening up new chances.

In the approaching battle between the GPUs and TPUs, there is a likelihood that quantum computing will go in the outside path. A key component in D-Wave's quantum computing is that it isn't really intended to solve each issue yet it is tending to a similar need in the preparing market that GPUs as of now satisfy. Google discharged a paper in which they find that there is an impressive computational bit of leeway when utilizing the D-Wave quantum computer over an old style processor. In numerous angles, a quantum computer can do something very similar a GPU can do, simply quicker, and these time is cash.

Quantum computing is proceeding to scale up, and with the ongoing declaration from the Vancouver based quantum computing organization, D-Wave, of their 2,000-qubit processor, it doesn't give indications of easing back down.

D-Wave is the central quantum computing organization that has made the technology accessible for business use. The quantum computing processors are in a direct challenge with the more custom kinds of chips utilized for Machine Learning and AI like GPUs and the recently declared second-age TPU from Google.

The significant piece of quantum computing is that it replaces the conventional perspective of computing. By supplanting the regular section, 0 or 1, with another kind of data, it opens up to exponential measures of potential outcomes. The qubit can be in the superposition state where it is neither +1 or - 1 yet, it could be said it is both, and it is this that takes into account the superfast computing.

The D-Wave quantum computers utilize the way toward toughening. This includes a progression of minuscule magnets to be orchestrated on a matrix. Each attractive field impacts one another, and afterward, they arrange themselves into a situation to limit the measure of vitality put away in the whole area. It is during this procedure that one can change the quality of the attractive area from every magnet with the goal that the attractions situate themselves in a manner to solve specific problems. To find a good pace, you start with high measures of vitality, so it is simple for the magnets to flip to and from. At that point, as you bring down the temperature, the attractions arrive at lower and lower levels of vitality until they are solidified into the most minimal vitality state. Here it is conceivable to peruse the direction of every magnet and discover the response to the issue. One can say that D-Wave's quantum computer is a sort of simple computer depending on Nature's algorithms to determine the design of the most reduced vitality state.

This is the place we luck out. This particular class of quantum computing happens to be helpful for a subset of streamlining computing problems, particularly those outfitted towards Machine Learning. Many Machine Learning problems can be reformulated as vitality problems. The D-Wave quantum computers are intended to help issues that need elevated level thinking, followed by decision making. Quantum computing considers Artificial Intelligence or AI frameworks to mimic human manners of thinking considerably more intently than an old-style processor. And keeping in mind that the possibility of quantum computing can be challenging to comprehend, its utilization in Machine Learning advance technology is unmistakably opening up new chances.

In the impending battle between the GPUs and TPUs, there is a likelihood that quantum computing will go on the outside path. A key component in D-Wave's quantum computing is that it isn't intended to solve each issue, yet it is tending to a similar need in the preparing market that GPUs as of now satisfy. Google discharged a paper in which they find that there is an impressive computational bit of leeway when utilizing the D-Wave quantum computer over an old-style processor. In numerous angles, a quantum computer can do something very similar a GPU can do, only.

Quantum Search

As discussed before, Grover's calculation plays out a pursuit over an unordered arrangement of N = 2n things to locate the interesting component that satisfies some condition. While the best old style calculation for an inquiry over unordered information requires O(N) time11, Grover's calculation plays out the pursuit on a quantum computer in just O(√N) activities, a quadratic speedup.

As Grover himself notes, if the calculation were to run in a limited intensity of O(lg N) steps, at that point it would give a calculation in BQP to problems in NPC. However, Grover's calculation doesn't give such a runtime, and is an asymptotically ideal arrangement, so no authoritative articulation can be made about the connection between the multifaceted nature classes BQP and NP dependent on the exhibition of Grover's calculation.

Grover's hunt calculation is a decent prologue to quantum algorithms since it exhibits how the characteristics of quantum frameworks can be utilized to enhance the lower runtime limits of traditional algorithms. So as to accomplish such a speedup, Grover depends on the quantum superposition of states. In the same way as other quantum algorithms, Grover's starts by placing the machine into an equivalent superposition of all conceivable 2n conditions of the n-qubit register. Recollect that implies there is an equivalent plenteousness of 1/√2 n related with each conceivable design of qubits in the framework, and an equivalent likelihood of 1/2 n that the framework will be in any of the 2n states.

These potential states relate to all the potential passages in Grover's database, thus beginning with equivalent amplitudes appointed to every component in the pursuit space, each component can be considered without a moment's delay in a quantum superposition, and amplitudes can be controlled from that point to deliver the right section in the database with a likelihood of "at any rate" 1/2.

Alongside the superposition of states, Grover's calculation, and all the more for the most part the group of quantum algorithms that utilization what is known as plenteousness enhancement, abuse the characteristics of quantum amplitudes that separate those amplitudes from straightforward probabilities. The way in to these algorithms is the particular moving of the period of one state of a quantum framework, one that satisfies some condition, at every cycle. Playing out a stage move of π is identical to duplicating the sufficiency of that state by −1: the adequacy for that state changes, yet the likelihood of being in that state continues as before (since the likelihood disregards the indication of the abundancy). Be that as it may, consequent changes performed on the framework exploit that distinction in sufficiency to single out that condition of varying stage and to eventually build the likelihood of the framework being in that state. Such arrangements of activities would not be conceivable if the amplitudes didn't hold that additional data with respect to the period of the state notwithstanding the likelihood. These abundancy enhancement algorithms are novel to quantum computing due to this nature of amplitudes that has no simple in old style probabilities.

Simon's algorithm: How it works

Given a capacity following up on n-bit strings, Simon's calculation starts by instating two n-bit registers to 0:

$|0\rangle^{\otimes n} |0\rangle^{\otimes n}$

At that point applying the Hadamard change to the primary register to achieve an equivalent superposition of states:

$$H^{\otimes n} |0\rangle |0\rangle = \frac{1}{\sqrt{2^n}} \sum_{x \in \{0,1\}^n} |x\rangle |0\rangle$$

Next, the given prophet work f(x) is questioned on both the registers. The prophet is actualized as a unitary activity that plays out the change Of(x) |xi |yi = |xi |f(x) ⊕yi. At the point when the prophet is approached the registers in the design depicted over, the outcome will be no change to the primary register, and f(x) put away in the second register, since f(x) ⊕ 0 = f(x):

$$\frac{1}{\sqrt{2^n}} \sum_{x \in \{0,1\}^n} |x\rangle |f(x)\rangle$$

Presently the subsequent register is estimated. There are two potential cases to consider in deciding the effect of that measurment on the primary register: either the XOR veil a = 0n or a = {0, 1} n. On the off chance that a = 0n , then f is injective: each estimation of x relates to aone of a kind worth f(x). This implies the main register stays in an equivalent superposition; Despite the deliberate estimation of f(x), x could be any piece string in {0, 1} n with equivalent. Then again, if a = {0, 1} n, estimating the subsequent register decides a solid estimation of f(x), call it f(z), which restricts the potential estimations of the main register.

By the meaning of the capacity f(x), there are actually two potential estimations of x with the end goal that f(x) = f(z): z and z ⊕ a. The condition of the primary register in the wake of estimating the second is along these lines diminished to an equivalent superposition of those two qualities:

$$\frac{1}{\sqrt{2}}|z\rangle + \frac{1}{\sqrt{2}}|z \oplus a\rangle$$

Since there will be no more activities on the subsequent register, further computations will concentrate just on the primary register. The subsequent stage is to isolate the data about a that is presently put away in the first register. This should be possible by applying the Hadamard change once more. Recollect that the Hadamard change might be characterized utilizing the bitwise dab item x · y as:

$$H^{\otimes n}|x\rangle = \frac{1}{\sqrt{2^n}} \sum_{y \in \{0,1\}^n} (-1)^{x \cdot y} |y\rangle$$

Using this notation, the result of applying a second Hadamard operation is:

$$H^{\otimes n}\left[\frac{1}{\sqrt{2}}|z\rangle + \frac{1}{\sqrt{2}}|z \oplus a\rangle\right]$$

$$= \frac{1}{\sqrt{2}}H^{\otimes n}|z\rangle + \frac{1}{\sqrt{2}}H^{\otimes n}|z \oplus a\rangle$$

$$= \frac{1}{\sqrt{2}}\left[\frac{1}{\sqrt{2^n}}\sum_{y\in\{0,1\}^n}(-1)^{z\cdot y}|y\rangle\right] + \frac{1}{\sqrt{2}}\left[\frac{1}{\sqrt{2^n}}\sum_{y\in\{0,1\}^n}(-1)^{(z\oplus a)\cdot y}|y\rangle\right]$$

$$= \frac{1}{\sqrt{2^{n+1}}}\sum_{y\in\{0,1\}^n}\left[(-1)^{z\cdot y} + (-1)^{(z\oplus a)\cdot y}\right]|y\rangle$$

$$= \frac{1}{\sqrt{2^{n+1}}}\sum_{y\in\{0,1\}^n}\left[(-1)^{z\cdot y} + (-1)^{(z\cdot y)\oplus(a\cdot y)}\right]|y\rangle$$

$$= \frac{1}{\sqrt{2^{n+1}}}\sum_{y\in\{0,1\}^n}(-1)^{z\cdot y}\left[1 + (-1)^{a\cdot y}\right]|y\rangle$$

Presently the estimation of the principal register is estimated. In the ruffian situation where a = 0n (f isinjective), a string will be created from {0, 1} n with uniform distribution.

For the situation where x ⊕ y = 0 6 n , notice that either a · y = 0 or a · y = 1. In the event that a · y = 1, at that point

Condition 19f becomes:

$$\frac{1}{\sqrt{2^{n+1}}}\sum_{y\in\{0,1\}^n}(-1)^{z\cdot y}\left[1 + (-1)^1\right]|y\rangle = \frac{1}{\sqrt{2^{n+1}}}\sum_{y\in\{0,1\}^n}(-1)^{z\cdot y}[0]|y\rangle$$

$$= 0|y\rangle$$

The sufficiency, and hence likelihood, that an estimation of y to such an extent that a · y = 1 is equivalent to 0, thus such a y will never be estimated. Realizing that it will consistently be valid that a · y = 0,

Condition 19f can be disentangled:

$$\frac{1}{\sqrt{2^{n+1}}} \sum_{y \in \{0,1\}^n} (-1)^{z \cdot y} \left[1 + (-1)^0\right] |y\rangle = \frac{2}{\sqrt{2^{n+1}}} \sum_{y \in \{0,1\}^n} (-1)^{z \cdot y} |y\rangle$$

$$= \frac{1}{\sqrt{2^{n-1}}} \sum_{y \in \{0,1\}^n} (-1)^{z \cdot y} |y\rangle$$

At the point when a $b = 0^n$, the aftereffect of estimating the principal register subsequent to playing out Simon's calculation will consistently create a string $y \in \{0, 1\}^n$: $a \cdot y = 0$. From Equation 21a, the abundancy related with each worth y is equivalent to $\pm \sqrt{2^{1-n}}$, giving the likelihood:

$$\left|\frac{1}{\sqrt{2^{n-1}}}\right|^2 = \left|\frac{-1}{\sqrt{2^{n-1}}}\right|^2 = \frac{1}{2^{n-1}}$$

of watching any of the strings y with the end goal that $a \cdot y = 0$, a uniform distribution over the 2^{n-1} strings that satisfy $a \cdot y = 0$.

On the off chance that Simon's calculation is executed n – multiple times, n – 1 strings $y_1, y_2, \ldots, y_{n-1} \in \{0, 1\}^n$ can be watched, which structure an arrangement of n – 1 direct conditions in n questions of the

structure:

$$y_1 \cdot a = y_{11}a_1 + y_{12}a_2 + \ldots + y_{1n}a_n = 0$$
$$y_2 \cdot a = y_{11}a_1 + y_{22}a_2 + \ldots + y_{2n}a_n = 0$$
$$\vdots$$
$$y_{n-1} \cdot a = y_{(n-1)1}a_1 + y_{(n-1)2}a_2 + \ldots + y_{(n-1)n}a_n = 0$$

To discover a from here is simply a question of unraveling for the n questions, each a piece in an, all together to decide an in general. Obviously, this requires an arrangement of n − 1 straightly autonomous conditions.

The likelihood of watching the principal string y0 is 21−n

. After another cycle of Simon's calculation, the likelihood of watching another distinct piece string would be 1 − 21−n . The likelihood of watching n − 1 distinct estimations of y in succession, thus a lower bound on the probability of obtaining n − 1 linearly independent equations, is:

$$\prod_{n=1}^{\infty} \left[1 - \frac{1}{2^n}\right] \approx .2887881 > \frac{1}{4}$$

So, a linearly independent system of n − 1 equations, and from there the value of a, can be obtained by repeating Simon's algorithm no more than 4n times. Simon's algorithm requires only O(n) queries to f in order to determine a, while classical algorithms require exponential time.

A considerable lot of the additionally intriguing quantum algorithms, for example, quantum reenacted toughening or on the other hand quantum Bayesian systems, require a significantly more careful comprehension of the basic math. In any case, with the new quantum worldview approaching out yonder, it never again bodes well for quantum calculation to be disregarded in the undergrad computer science educational plan. Ideally, the investigation of quantum algorithms will soon be ordinary. Up to that point, this instructional exercise in any event shows that basic quantum algorithms are not outside the ability to comprehend of the normal undergrad computer science understudy, giving a delicate prologue to the nuts and bolts of quantum calculation to the undergrad populace.

Classical circuits

In classical intricacy theory, a Boolean circuit is a nite coordinated non-cyclic diagram with AND, OR, and NOT doors. It has n input hubs, which contain the n input bits (n 0). The inner hubs are AND, OR, and NOT doors, and there are at least one assigned yield hubs. The underlying information bits are nourished into AND, OR, and NOT doors as indicated by the circuit, and in the end the yield hubs expect some worth. We state that a circuit processes some Boolean capacity f: f0; 1gn ! f0; 1gm if the yield hubs get the correct worth f(x) for each info x 2 f0; 1gn.

A circuit family is a set C = fCng of circuits, one for each info size n. Each circuit has one yield bit. Such a family perceives or chooses a language L f0; 1g = [n 0f0; 1gn if, for each n and each info x 2 f0;

1^gn, the circuit C_n yields 1 if $x \in L$ and yields 0 otherwise. Such a circuit family is consistently polynomial if there is a deterministic Turing machine that yields C_n given n as info, utilizing space logarithmic in n.1 Note that the size (number of entryways) of the circuits C_n would then be able to develop all things considered polynomially with n. It is realized that consistently polynomial circuit families are equivalent in capacity to polynomial-time deterministic Turing machines: a language L can be chosen by a consistently polynomial circuit family I $L \in P$ [118, Theorem 11.5], where P is the class of dialects decidable by polynomial-time Turing machines.

Additionally, we can think about randomized circuits. These get, notwithstanding the n input bits, additionally some arbitrary bits (\coin ips") as info. A randomized circuit registers a capacity f on the off chance that it effectively yields the correct answer f(x) with likelihood in any event $2/3$ for each x (likelihood assumed control over the estimations of the irregular bits; the $2/3$ might be supplanted by any $1/2 + $"). Randomized circuits are equivalent in capacity to randomized Turing machines: a language L can be chosen by a consistently

polynomial randomized circuit family I $L \in BPP$, where BPP (\Bounded-blunder Probabilistic Polynomial time") is the class of dialects that can be perceived by randomized Turing machines with progress likelihood in any event $2/3$.

Quantum circuits

A quantum circuit (additionally called quantum system or quantum entryway exhibit) sums up the possibility of classical circuit families, supplanting the AND, OR, and NOT doors by rudimentary quantum doors. A quantum entryway is a unitary change on a little (generally 1, 2, or 3) number of qubits. We saw various models as of now in the past section: the bit ip entryway X, the stage ip door Z, the Hadamard door H. The fundamental 2-qubit door we have seen is the controlled-NOT (CNOT) entryway. Including another control register, we get the 3-qubit Tooli entryway, additionally called controlled-controlled-not (CCNOT) door. This refutes the third piece of its information if both of the rst two bits are 1. The Tooli door is significant on the grounds that it is finished for classical reversible calculation: any classical calculation can be actualized by a circuit of Tooli entryways. This is anything but difficult to see: utilizing helper wires with xed values, To oli can execute AND (x the third ingoing wire to 0) and NOT (x the first and second ingoing wire to 1). It is realized that and NOT-entryways together suce to execute any classical Boolean circuit, so on the off chance that we can apply (or reenact) To oli doors, we can actualize any classical calculation in a reversible way.

Numerically, such basic quantum doors can be created into greater unitary tasks by taking tensor items (if entryways are applied in corresponding to different parts of the register), and conventional grid items (if entryways are applied successively). We have just observed a basic case of such a circuit of basic entryways in the past part, in particular to actualize teleportation.

For example, if we apply the Hadamard gate H to each bit in a register of n zeroes, we obtain

$$\frac{1}{2^{n/p}} \sum_{j \in \{0,1\}^n} |j\rangle$$

Quantum Computing and Healthcare Technology

Envision leading a MRI, on a solitary cell rather than the entire body - snapping a photo of the atom or only a gathering of particles inside the phone, distinguishing and inspecting the issue territories inside DNA, and concocting an increasingly precise diagnosis and patient treatment. This is conceivable today through the precision of Quantum Computing and Nanotechnology incorporated with a MRI hardware.

In an ongoing news discharge IBM proclaimed that they are exceptionally near make an achievement in the domains of Quantum computing. Because of some exploratory triumphs they are nearer to fabricate the primary Quantum Computer, that can exploit the peculiarities of quantum material science and could solve certain problems in a moment or two, that would otherwise take present-day computers billions of years to solve.

Quantum computing is a computing framework dependent on qubits rather than bits; where qubits (Quantum Bits) are essential units of data in a quantum computer. While a piece can speak to only one of two potential outcomes, for example, 0 or 1, or yes or not, Qubits can speak to a lot more choices: 0 or 1, 1 and 0, the event of different mixes of Qubits, and that too at the same time.

In this way, Qubit speaks to a variety of potential outcomes and all can be determined at the same time considering.

The Qubit idea manages little particles (subatomic particles). It has been demonstrated that a subatomic molecule can have various states at the same time in light of the fact that the particles are rarely static. This is apparent on the grounds that they move extremely quick, near the speed of light. In this way, a molecule condition of the molecule (Qubit) appears to be unique to various eyewitnesses and the molecule has a few states all the while. That is the reason one subatomic molecule can have various states and probabilities, simultaneously. We can utilize it to supplant bits and show signs of improvement execution: Much better execution! And afterward, when you join Qubits, that blend holds an exponentially bigger measure of data than bits. Subatomic logic is significantly more dominant than paired logic utilized in typical computing.

Accordingly, you can process muddled data quicker. Its principle applications are encryption, unscrambling, displaying, databases, voice acknowledgment, structure acknowledgment, recreation and computerized reasoning, in addition to numerous others yet non-existent applications.

Envision its usage and impact in the domain of Healthcare, explicitly e-Health. Volumes of electronically accessible Patient information, organized, displayed, recreated, and handled in portions of seconds - man-made brainpower for diagnosis and condition consistency with practically 100% exactness, will increase a great many crease, outperforming unthought-of points of confinement.

Quantum Computing has additionally demonstrated that two ensnared particles share its existence. That is the point at which one alters its express, the other additionally changes its own state at the same time, regardless of how far they are known to man. That implies we can "transport" data starting with one spot then onto the next without physical development, just by adjusting one caught molecule state.

In e-Health, this could mean programmed remote and solid diagnosis, with electronic patient data, through quick correspondence with caught subatomic particles. What's more, with nano-scale precision applications, this is only a glimpse of something larger.

A New Era in Super-Computing?

In case you're searching for zones in which maths can be applied to this present reality, look no farther than computing and specifically the most recent energizing advances originating from colleges in the US. At a gathering of the American Physical Society in Dallas, scientists from University of California, Santa Barbara have been showing the most recent strides making a course for a quantum computer.

A quantum computer, something that, apparently, presently can't seem to be assembled, would have the option to perform counts on a scale that would unfathomably out-play out the present super-computers.

The UCSB gadget is one stage along the street towards such a computer. It houses a chip containing 9 quantum gadgets, four of which are "quantum bits" or Qubits, which do the estimations. In the not so distant future, the group plans to expand the quantity of Qubits to 10. At the point when scientists can build the quantity of Qubits to around 100, they figure the chip will be the basis of a reasonable, usable computer.

The entirety of this opens the likelihood that sooner rather than later we'll have the intensity of the present super-computers on our work areas, on our laps, even in our cell phones.

For these improvements, we owe a great deal to Erwin Schrödinger, whose work on quantum material science and wave condition made ready for the bizarre universe of quantum mechanics.

At its heart, quantum computing relies upon "super-position", which is the apparently unnatural capacity for a molecule to be in two states simultaneously. A molecule turning one way could be given a powerless beat of vitality, which may be sufficient to set it turning the other way, however perhaps not. For whatever length of time that the molecule is not being watched or associated with in any capacity, quantum material science says that the molecule is in the two states simultaneously.

Presently, we could utilize an entire line of these particles to speak to the paired digits of a number. On the off chance that an estimation is performed utilizing a conventional computer, we would need to sustain each number into the computer independently. But since a quantum computer can work on particles in super-position, it can play out the figuring on all the potential blends at the same time. A number whose paired portrayal is 7 digits in length is somewhere in the range of 0 and 127. A customary computer would need to do a count on every one of these 127 numbers. A quantum computer could do them at the same time.

Be that as it may, the intensity of quantum computing brings colossal difficulties for society. Actually, as things stand, a completely working quantum computer would imperil the dependability of the world. This is on the grounds that world business relies upon the utilization of secure figures to ensure and confirm monetary exchanges. Moreover, many secure discussions among governments and government organizations are completed utilizing similar arrangements of figures. With the impossible computing power that quantum computing would bring, these figures, which we have recently thought to be unbreakable, would be rendered futile.

So the race is on: will the quantum computer show up first, presenting dangers to global security and trade? Or then again will another quantum cryptography be grown first, verifying exchanges in another unbreakable way? (It's another story, however such a type of encryption has just been indicated conceivable over short correspondence distances. What's more, it is completely unbreakable.)

Limitations Of Quantum Computing

Note that the field of quantum computing is still in its early stages. [10] Many constraints related with it have been found in different trials, some of which are as follows:

Quantum Decoherence

Quantum decoherence is the loss of requesting between stage points, frequently because of the obstruction of the quantum frame work under perception with outside impacts. The very certainty that quantum computers should be isolated from outside frameworks to work appropriately represents an issue, as evident isolation is exceptionally hard to accomplish. Indeed, even a wanderer attractive field can incredibly influence the yield of a quantum computer.

Acquiring a Valid Output

A significant confinement of quantum computers lies in getting a deliberate yield esteem that relates to one of the basis conditions of the qubits. Structuring the logical activities expected to accomplish this is trying, as a quantum framework can be in countless superpositions of various states at a specific moment. Not these can be estimated; just the yields comparing to the basis states are quantifiable.

Countless calculations may must be performed utilizing a quantum computer before a right yield is gotten, henceforth decreasing the speed of the procedure. The way that in any event, watching a qubit may change its state further mixes the issue.

Quantum Reenactment

Feynman's unique vision of quantum computing depended on its incentive for reenacting complex quantum mechanical frameworks, and this remaining parts a territory of dynamic intrigue. For quite a long time, regular computer reenactments have extended our comprehension of quantum mechanical frameworks, however the multifaceted nature of these reproductions has constrained them to utilize approximations that eventually limit the measure of valuable data we can separate. The essential trouble is the equivalent certainty that makes quantum computers compelling: depicting a quantum framework requires various parameters that develops exponentially with the size of the quantum frameworks.

Quantum computers are undeniably fit to reenact quantum mechanical frameworks in an assortment of disciplines, including quantum chemistry, materials science, atomic physical science, and dense issue material science.

The Boston Consulting Group has assessed that improved quantum reenactment could have a market estimation of several billions of dollars to pharmaceutical organizations alone.

Quantum reenactment (counting chemistry, cross section QCD, material science, and so on.) right now represents an enormous part of supercomputer time, and we expect that quantum computers would not only have the option to accomplish these recreations all the more efficiently yet additionally enormously grow the scope of what is conceivable with them Several quantum reproduction algorithms have just been proposed and tried on quantum computers. These underlying algorithms have been intended for frameworks requiring insignificant resources. One promising ebb and flow line of research is half and half quantum-classical methodologies. These methodologies off-load certain calculations onto classical computers, for example Hamiltonian integrals can be pre-registered on a classical computer and afterward stacked into the quantum computer calculation as parameters. On the other hand, a quantum computer could be utilized to speedup basic parts in reenactments, e.g.,giving data around two-molecule thickness networks.

Ground-state properties are commonly acquired utilizing variational methods. These are iterative techniques where in one picks an underlying wave work contingent upon at least one parameters, and afterward decide parameter esteems that endeavor to limit the normal vitality esteems. The subsequent wave work is an upper bound on ground state vitality. Emphasis (for example by means of angle plunge) can keep on improving the gauge.

In the future, we expect there to be a solid requirement for new algorithms as the quantity of qubits and accessible number of entryway tasks increment, since we will never again be compelled to limit assets. Quantum computers are expected to have the option to reenact properties of energized states and elements just as ground states. Most classical abdominal muscle initio codes (i.e., those depending on essential normal laws without extra suspicions or uncommon models) are constrained to recreating static properties of ground states. There is additionally a requirement for new changes mapping molecule frameworks obeying either fermionic and bosonic statistics onto registers of distinguishable quantum bits that may be compelled by specific equipment networks.

Past material science recreations themselves, there are likewise openings in related subject regions including protein displaying, atomic elements, climate expectation, liquid mechanics, tranquilize plan, and computational optics. By utilizing QCs for the classically-unmanageable segments of industrially important problems in sedate structure or different fields, QCs of adequate scale and dependability have the potential for critical business pertinence groupings of activities. Thusly, to some associated with QEC research, QEC itself is the essential remaining task at hand that will be running on QCs of the future. Future research is required to create QEC approaches that are viable and asset effective, so they can be utilized sooner (ie at lower qubit checks) in the technology course of events.

AI and Optimization

Significantly less is thought about the utility of quantum computers for AI, however the significance of the application makes this a convincing region of study. On the off chance that we can deliver high dimensional super positions containing either the pertinent information or some nonlinear capacity of it, at that point we can rapidly perform bunching, PCA, and other information analysis assignments. Be that as it may, this underlying state planning is as yet an obstacle. Getting a helpful in general speedup will require setting up a condition of 2n measurements in significantly less than 2n time, ideally in poly(n) time. We presently just skill to do that in some uncommon cases36. It would be of extraordinary utility to extend the scope of situations where this is conceivable.

Variational and adiabatic algorithms for streamlining and characterization can run on close term quantum computers and however are far from classical simulators37. Despite the fact that these approaches show promising focal points in quantum chemistry what's more, simulation38, they have not yet provably outflanked the most popular classical algorithms. Experimental proof from running them on close term quantum computers will improve our understanding for longer-term and progressively adaptable methodologies.

Quantum Teleportation And Quantum Theory Of Information

Data is physical, and any handling of data is constantly performed by physical methods a blameless sounding explanation, however its results are definitely not inconsequential. Over the most recent couple of years there has been a blast of hypothetical and test advancements prompting the production of a major new discipline: a distinctly Quantum Theory of Information. Quantum material science permits the development of subjectively new kinds of logic entryways, completely secure cryptosystems (frameworks that consolidate interchanges and cryptography), the packing of two bits of data into one physical piece and, has far quite recently been proposed, a child of "teleportation".

As of not long ago teleportation was not paid attention to by scientists. For the most part teleportation is the name given by science fiction essayists to the accomplishment of making an article or then again individual disintegrate in one spot while an ideal copy shows up elsewhere.

Regularly this is finished by filtering the article so as to extricate all the data from it, at that point this data is transmitted to the data from it, at that point this data is transmitted to the accepting area and used to develop the copy, not really from the real material of the first, however likely from molecules of the same sorts, orchestrated in the very same example as the first. A teleportation machine would resemble a fax machine, then again, actually it would chip away at 3-dimensional items also as reports, it would create a precise rather an inexact copy and it would pulverize the first during the time spent filtering it.

In classical material science, an item can be transported, on a basic level by playing out a estimation to totally describe the properties of the item that data can at that point be sent to another area, and this article remade. In addition classical data theory concurs with ordinary instinct: if a message is to be sent utilizing an object which can be placed into one of N distinguishable states, the most extreme number of various messages which can be sent is N. For instance, single photon can have just two distinguishable polarization states: left gave and right gave. In this manner a solitary photon can not transmit in excess of two distinguishable messages for example one piece of data.

Despite the fundamental inquiry: is it conceivable to give a total reproduction of the first article? The appropriate response is no. All the physical frameworks are eventually quantum mechanical and quantum mechanics discloses to us that it is difficult to totally decide the condition of an obscure quantum framework, making it difficult to utilize the classical estimation method to move a quantum framework starting with one area then onto the next. This is because of Heisenberg Uncertainty Principle which expresses that all the more precisely an item is examined, the more it is disturbed by the filtering procedure, until one arrives at a point where the articles unique state has been totally disrupted, still without having removed enough data to make an ideal imitation. This seems like a strong contention against 18 teleportation: in the event that one can't separate enough data from an item to make an ideal duplicate, it would be seen that an ideal duplicate can't be made.

Charles H Bennet with his gathering and Stephen Wiesner have proposed an exceptional strategy for transporting quantum states utilizing EPR states (caught states). Quantum teleportation might be portrayed conceptually as far as two particles, An and B. A currently possesses an obscure state $|\psi\rangle$ spoke to as:

$$|\psi\rangle = \alpha|0\rangle + \beta|1\rangle$$

This is a solitary quantum bit (qubit)- a two level quantum frameworks. The point of teleportation is to move the state $|\psi\rangle$ from A to B. This is accomplished by utilizing snared states. An and B every gang one qubit of a two qubit caught state;

$$|\psi\rangle(|0\rangle_A |0\rangle_B) + |1\rangle_A|1\rangle_B)$$

The above state can be reworked in the Bell basis $(|00\rangle\pm|11\rangle)$, $(|01\rangle\pm|10\rangle)$ for the initial two qubit and a contingent unitary change of the state $|\psi\rangle$ for the last one, that is

$$(|00\rangle+|11\rangle)|\psi\rangle+(|00\rangle-|11\rangle)\sigma Z|\psi\rangle + (|01\rangle+|10\rangle)\sigma X |\psi\rangle + (|01\rangle-|10\rangle)(-i\sigma Y|\psi\rangle)$$

Where σX, σY, σZ are Pauli lattices in the $|0\rangle$, $|1\rangle$ basis. An estimation is performed on A's qubits in the Bell basis. Contingent upon the results of these estimations, B's particular states are $|\psi\rangle$, σZ $|\psi\rangle$, σX $|\psi\rangle$, - iσZ $|\psi\rangle$ A sends the result of its estimation to B, who would then be able to recuperate the first state $|\psi\rangle$ by applying the proper unitary change I, σZ, σ Y or iσY relying upon An's estimation result. It might be noticed that quantum state transmission has not been accomplished quicker than light since B must sit tight for An's estimation result to land before he can recoup the quantum state.

Thermodynamics Of Quantum Computation

Computers are machines and like all machines they are dependent upon thermodynamics imperatives, in view of the laws of thermodynamics. Closely resembling any physical framework, the present day computers dependent on advanced gadgets produce heat in activity. The fundamental inquiry is: Can computerized computers be improved in order to limit generation of warmth. It turns out that it is conceivable to think (consistent with the laws of material science) of a perfect computer equipped for molding, keeping up and moving around advanced signs, keeping up and moving around advanced signs with no warmth age. All things considered there is one place where warmth must be delivered. At whatever point data is eradicated the stage space related with the framework that stores data recoils. Eradicating a solitary piece of data lessens entropy of the framework that put away that data by in any event $\Delta S=k\log 2$. This decrease of entropy brings about warmth move to the earth.

In this way if a computer could be built that doesn't delete any data, such a computer could work without producing any warmth whatsoever. This is precisely the circumstance in quantum computers. Quantum Computation is reversible (however not the read out of the consequence of that calculation). It is hence conceivable, in any event on a basic level, to carryout quantum calculation without producing heat. Obviously, as a general rule the computer would still produce a ton of warmth. Electric heartbeats moving along copper wires would need to work their way against resistance. Electrons diffusing from a source would at present slam into precious stone defects and with electrons in the channel once more, producing heat. In any case, at any rate in perfect circumstance, copper wires could be supplanted with superconductors, defective gems with official ones.

The reversibility of quantum computers is being acknowledged by imagining and creating exceptional doors. In computerized computers door like NOR, AND, NAND and XOR are utilized. Every one of these entryways are irreversible: they should create heat. Measure of data on the correct hand side of

(a,b) (a∧b

is not exactly the measure of data on the left hand side. Utilizing Toffoli entryways Charles Bennett has shown that quantum computers are fit for playing out any calculation using just reversible advances. These exceptional doors keep up all data that is passed to them, with the goal that the calculation can be run forward and in reverse.

Thus, the calculation brings about a lot of information, because each middle of the road step is recollected, yet heat age is dispensed with which the calculation goes on. After the calculation is over the calculation can be run in reverse to reestablish the underlying condition of the computer and stay away from its sudden ignition.

Test Realization of Quantum Computer

The engineering straightforwardness makes the quantum computer quicker, littler and less expensive be that as it may, its reasonable complexities are presenting troublesome problems for its test acknowledgment. All things considered various endeavors have been made toward this path with an 20empowering achievement. It is envisaged that it may not be too far when the quantum computer would supplant advanced computer with its full possibilities. A portion of the endeavors for the trial acknowledgment of quantum computer are abridged as follows:

Heteropolymers:

The first heteropolymer based quantum computer was planned and worked in 1988 by Teich and afterward improved by Lloyd in 1993. In a heteropolymer computer a direct exhibit of particles is utilized as memory cells. Data is put away on a cell by siphoning the relating particle into an energized state. Guidelines are transmitted to the heteropolymer by laser beats of fittingly tuned frequencies. The idea of the calculation that is performed on chosen iotas is controlled by the shape and the span of the beat.

Ion Traps:

A particle trap quantum computer was first proposed by Cirac and Zoller in 1995 and executed first by Monroe and partners in 1995 and afterward by Schwarzchild in 1996. The particle trap computer encodes information in vitality conditions of particles and in vibrational modes between the particles. Theoretically every particle is worked by a different laser. A fundamental analysis exhibited that Fourier changes can be assessed with the particle trap computer. This, thusly, prompts Shor's considering calculation, which is based on Fourier changes.

Quantum Electrodynamics Cavity:

A quantum electrodynamics (QED) cavity computer was shown by Turchette and teammates in 1995. The computer consists of a QED pit filled with some cesium particles and a course of action of lasers, stage move identifiers, polarizer also, mirrors. The arrangement is a genuine quantum computer since it can make, control what's more, protect superposition and traps.

Nuclear Magnetic Resonance:

A Nuclear Magnetic Resonance (NMR) computer consists of a case loaded up with a fluid and a NMR machine. Every atom in the fluid is a free quantum memory register. Calculation continues by sending radio heartbeats to the test and perusing its reaction. Qubits are actualized as turn conditions of the cores of particles comprising the atoms. In a NMR computer the readout of the memory register is accomplished by an estimation performed on a statistical outfit of state, 2.7x10 19 particles. This is as opposed to QED pit computer particle trap computer, in which a solitary isolated quantum framework was utilized for memory register.

NMR computer can solve NP (Non-polynomial) complete problems in polynomial time. Most functional accomplishments in quantum computing so far have been accomplished utilizing NMR computers.

Quantum Dots

Quantum computers dependent on quantum speck technology utilize more straightforward engineering and less sophisticated test, hypothetical and numerical abilities when contrasted with the four quantum computer usage discussed up until now. A variety of quantum specks, in which the dabs are associated with their closest neighbors by the methods for gated burrowing boundaries are utilized for creating quantum entryways utilizing split door procedure. This conspire has one of the fundamental focal points: the qubits are controlled electrically. The disadvantage of this engineering is that quantum dabs can speak with their closest neighbors just coming about information read out is very troublesome.

Josephson Junctions

The Josephson intersection quantum computer was exhibited in 1999 by Nakamura what's more, the colleagues. In this computer a Cooper pair box, which is a little superconducting island anode is feebly coupled to a mass superconductor. Feeble coupling between the superconductors make a Josephson intersection between them which carries on as a capacitor. In the event that the Cooper box is little as a quantum speck, the charging current breaks into discrete move of individual Cooper sets, so at last it is conceivable to simply move a solitary Cooper pair over the intersection. Like quantum dab, computers in Josephson intersection computers, qubits are controlled electrically. Josephson intersection's quantum computers are one of the promising possibility for future advancements.

The Kane Computer

This computer looks similar to a quantum speck computer yet in different manners it is more like a NMR computer. It consists of a solitary attractively dynamic core of p 31in a gem of isotropically clean attractively idle Si 28. The example is then set in a exceptionally solid attractive field so as to set the turn of p 31equal or antiparallel with the bearing of the field. The turn of the p31core would then be able to be controlled by applying a radio recurrence heartbeat to a control anode, called A-door, neighboring the core.

Electron intervened communication between twists could thusly be controlled by applying voltage to terminals called J-entryways, set between the p 31cores.

Topological Quantum Computer

In this computer qubits are encoded in an arrangement of anyons. "Anyons" are quasiparticles in 2-dimensional media obeying parastatistics (neither Fermi Dirac nor Bose Einstein). In any case, in a way anyons are still nearer to fermions, on the grounds that a fermion like repugnance exists between them. The separate development of anyons is portrayed by interlace gathering. The thought behind the topological quantum computer is to utilize the plait bunch properties that portray the movement of anyons so as to complete quantum calculations. It is asserted that such a computer ought to be resistant to quantum mistakes of the topological strength of anyons.

Future Directions of Quantum Computing

The establishment of the subject of quantum calculation has gotten settled, be that as it may, everything else required for its future development is under investigation. That spreads quantum algorithms, getting elements and control of decoherence, nuclear scale technology and advantageous applications. Reversibility of quantum calculation may help in taking care of NP problems, which are simple one way yet hard in the contrary sense.

Worldwide minimization problems may profit by obstruction (as found in Fermat's rule in wave mechanics). Mimicked strengthening techniques may improve due to quantum burrowing through boundaries. Ground-breaking properties of complex numbers(analytic capacities, conformal mappings) may give new algorithms.

Quantum field theory can stretch out quantum calculation to take into account creation and devastation of quanta. The characteristic setting for such tasks is in quantum optics. For model, the customary twofold cut trial (or pillar splitter) can be seen as the duplicate activity. It is allowed in quantum theory in light of the fact that the power of the two duplicates is a large portion of the past worth. Hypothetical apparatuses for dealing with many-body quantum trap are not very much created. Its improved portrayal may create better execution of quantum logic doors and potential outcomes to address corresponded blunders.

In spite of the fact that decoherence can be depicted as a powerful procedure, its elements is definitely not comprehended. To have the option to control decoherence, one ought to have the option to make sense of the eigen states supported by nature in a given arrangement. The elements of estimation process is not seen either, much following a very long while of quantum mechanics.

Estimation is simply depicted as a non-unitary projection administrator in an otherwise unitary quantum theory. At last both the framework and the spectator are comprised of quantum building squares, and a bound together quantum portrayal of both estimation and decoherence must be created. Aside from hypothetical increase, it would help in improving the indicators that work near the quantum furthest reaches of perception. For physicist, it is of incredible enthusiasm to consider the change from classical to quantum system. Growth of the framework from tiny to mesoscopic levels, and decrease of nature from naturally visible to mesoscopic levels, can take us there. On the off chance that there is something past quantum theory hiding there, it would be seen in the battle for making quantum gadgets. We may discover new confinements of quantum theory in attempting to win decoherence.

Hypothetical improvements alone will be nothing more than trouble without a coordinating technology. These days, the race for scaling down of electronic circuits is not far away from the quantum truth of nature. To devise new kinds of instruments we should change our perspective from scientific to technological- quantum impacts are not for just perception, we ought to figure out how to control them from down to earth use. The future is not anticipated at this point, yet it is certainly promising.

Simon Edwards

Modern Cryptography

for Beginners

A Complete Guide to Discover
History, Features, Developments and Applications of Modern Cryptography

Copyright © 2020 publishing.

All rights reserved.

Author: Simon Edwards

No part of this publication may be reproduced, distributed or transmitted in any form or by any means, including photocopying recording or other electronic or mechanical methods or by any information storage and retrieval system without the prior written permission of the publisher, except in the case of brief quotation embodies in critical reviews and certain other non-commercial uses permitted by copyright law.

Chapter One

Introduction to Modern Cryptography

From Oxford Dictionary (2006) defines cryptography as the craft of composing or understanding codes. This definition might be generally precise, however it doesn't catch the pith of modern cryptography. To begin with, it centers exclusively around the issue of secret communication. This is prove by the way that the definition species \codes", somewhere else denned as \a arrangement of pre-masterminded signals, particularly used to guarantee mystery in transmitting messages". Second, the definition alludes to cryptography as a fine art. In reality, until the twentieth century (and apparently until late in that century), cryptography was a craftsmanship. Building great codes, or breaking existing ones, depended on inventiveness and individual aptitude. There was next to no hypothesis that could be depended upon and there was not in any case a well denned thought of what establishes great code.

In the late twentieth century, this image of cryptography drastically changed. A rich hypothesis developed, empowering the thorough investigation of cryptography as a science. Moreover, the of cryptography currently envelops substantially more than secret communication, including message authentication, digital signatures, protocols for exchanging secret keys, authentication protocols, electronic auctions and elections, and digital cash. Truth be told, modern cryptography can be said to be worried about issues that may emerge in any disseminated calculation that may go under interior or outer assault. Without endeavoring to give an ideal de country of modern cryptography, we would state that it is the logical investigation of strategies for making sure about digital data, exchanges, and appropriated calculations.

Another significant distinction between old style cryptography (state, before the 1980s) and modern cryptography identifies with who utilizes it. Verifiably, the significant buyers of cryptography were military and insight associations. Today, be that as it may, cryptography is all over the place! Security components that depend on cryptography are an essential piece of practically any PC framework. Clients (regularly accidentally) depend on cryptography each time they get to a made sure about site. Cryptographic techniques are utilized to authorize get to control in multi-client working frameworks, and to keep hoodlums from removing competitive advantages from taken PCs. Programming assurance strategies utilize encryption, authentication, and different apparatuses to forestall replicating. The rundown continues forever.

So, cryptography has gone from a fine art that managed secret communication for the military to science that assists with making sure about frameworks for conventional individuals the whole way across the globe. This likewise implies cryptography is turning into an increasingly more focal subject inside software engineering.

The focal point of this book is modern cryptography. However, we will start our examination by looking at the condition of cryptography before the progressions referenced previously. Other than permitting us to slide into the material, it will likewise give a comprehension of where cryptography has originated from with the goal that we can later perceive the amount it has changed. The investigation of "old style cryptography" | packed with impromptu developments of codes, and moderately straightforward approaches to break them fills in as great inspiration for the more thorough methodology we will be taking in the remainder of the book.

As noted above, cryptography was truly worried about secret communication. In particular, cryptography was worried about the development of figures (presently called encryption plans) for giving secret communication between two gatherings sharing some data ahead of time. The setting wherein the imparting parties share some secret data ahead of time is presently known as the private key (or the symmetric-key) setting. Before portraying some chronicled figures, we talk about the private-key setting and encryption in increasingly broad terms.

In the private-key setting, two gatherings share some secret data called a key, and utilize this key when they wish to discuss secretly with one another. A gathering communicating something specific uses the key to scramble (or \scramble") the message before it is sent, and the beneficiary uses a similar key to unscramble (or \unscramble") and recuperate the message upon receipt. The message itself is regularly called the plaintext, and the \scrambled" data that is really transmitted from the sender to the collector is known as the ciphertext; see Figure 1.1. The mutual key serves to recognize the imparting parties from whatever other gatherings who might be listening stealthily on their communication (which is accepted to happen over an open channel).

We stress that right now, same key is utilized to change over the plaintext into a ciphertext and back. This clarifies why this setting is otherwise called the symmetric-key setting, where the evenness lies in the way that the two gatherings hold a similar key which is utilized for both encryption and decoding. This is as opposed to the setting of hilter kilter encryption (presented in Chapter 9), where the sender and recipient don't share any secrets and di erent keys are utilized for encryption and decoding. The private-key setting is the exemplary one, as we will see later right now.

A certain supposition in any framework utilizing private-key encryption is that the imparting parties have some method for at first sharing a key in a secret way. (Note that in the event that one gathering essentially sends the key to the next over the open channel, a busybody acquires the key as well!) In military settings, this is certainly not an extreme issue since imparting parties can genuinely meet in a safe area so as to concur upon a key. In numerous modern settings, nonetheless, parties can't orchestrate any such physical gathering. As we will find in Chapter 9, this is a wellspring of extraordinary concern and really restricts the relevance of cryptographic frameworks that depend entirely on private-key techniques. In spite of this, there are as yet numerous settings where private-key strategies sauce and are in wide use; one model is circle encryption, where a similar client (at various focuses in time) utilizes a fixed secret key to both write to and read from the plate. As we will investigate further in Chapter, private-key encryption is additionally generally utilized related to uneven strategies.

The punctuation of encryption. We currently make the above conversation more formal. A private-key encryption plan, or figure, is contained three algorithms: the rest is a strategy for creating keys, the second a methodology for encoding, and the third a technique for decoding. These algorithms have the accompanying usefulness:

The key-age algorithm Gen is a probabilistic algorithm that out-puts a key k picked by some dissemination that is controlled by the plan.

The encryption algorithm Enc takes as info a key k and a plaintext m and yields a ciphertext c. We signify the encryption of the plaintext m utilizing the key k by Enck (m).

Types of Cryptography

Cryptographic systems have been being used since the hour of the Sumerians (3500 BCE). Cryptography depends on secret keys, which, as you'll review, are the contribution to the algorithm that delivers the ciphertext. There are two fundamental sorts of cryptography: customary cryptography and public-key cryptography. In ordinary cryptography, a solitary key is utilized to perform both encryption and decryption. Since the keys are indistinguishable, they're alluded to as symmetric keys. Since just one key is utilized in customary cryptography, it's less secure. On the off chance that somebody other than the planned beneficiary finds the key, he can decode the first message. Another disadvantage to traditional cryptography is that it's dangerous to appropriate. On the off chance that somebody captures the key on its way to the planned beneficiary, the security of the message is undermined. PGP Desktop additionally permits you to scramble singular documents and organizers, a part of your hard plate assigned as a virtual circle, or your whole hard circle.

In public-key cryptography, two particular keys are utilized a public key to perform encryption and a private key to perform decryption. Since the keys are unique, they're alluded to as lopsided keys. This permits anybody to encode a message yet just people with the comparing private key to decode messages. To explain, we should take a gander at a model. In the event that Paul needs to make an impression on Sara, he utilizes Sara's public key to encode the message. When Sara gets the message, she utilizes her private key to decode it. For whatever length of time that every individual in the message circle keeps his/her private key completely private, just the proposed beneficiary can decode the message. Public cryptography additionally conquers the conveyance issue in light of the fact that solitary public keys should be sent over the shaky system; private keys are looked after locally.

Next, we should direct our concentration toward a viable case of public-key cryptography. In the accompanying areas, we'll utilize an example application, PGP Desktop, to tell you the best way to create a public/private key pair to make sure about both email and texts. We will additionally tell you the best way to distribute your public key to the PGP Global Directory so others can send encoded messages to you. At the point when your machine returns on the web, the PGP Setup Assistant dispatches consequently. This utility encourages you complete introductory arrangement, including producing another key pair and alternatively distributing your public key to the PGP Global Directory. Note that you should finish the PGP Setup Assistant assignments preceding utilizing the essential application itself. Since PGP is introduced for all clients of course, you have to empower it for every window account exclusively. This implies you have to initially sign in with the proper Windows account, and afterward empower PGP for the dynamic account.

Computer Cryptography

Cryptography is the study of changing messages to make them secure and resistant to assault. The strict importance of cryptography is "secret composition". In the event that the first message is sent through a system, at that point any programmer can get access and change its significance. To guarantee the security of the message, the first message is changed to ciphertext utilizing an encryption algorithm by the sender. What's more, the collector utilizes a decryption algorithm to change the ciphertext once more into plaintext.

Encryption and decryption algorithms are called figures. Furthermore, those algorithms work on a lot of numbers called Key. To scramble a message, we need an encryption algorithm, encryption key and the plain content. These make the ciphertext. Thus, to decode a message, we need a decryption algorithm, decryption key and the ciphertext. These uncover the plaintext. In cryptography three characters (Alice, Bob, and Eve) are extremely famous. Alice is the individual who sends message and Bob is the beneficiary. Eve upsets this communication by blocking message to reveal the information.

There are 2 sorts of figures (cryptography algorithms)

1-Symmetric-key or Secret key Cryptography

2-Asymmetric-key or Public key Cryptography

Symmetric-Key Cryptography

In Symmetric-Key Cryptography, a similar key is utilized by both sender and collector. So the key must be known to the two gatherings. The conventional figures are substitution figure and transposition figure. A substitution figure substitutes one image with another. For instance, we can supplant character B with G and F with X. In a transposition figure, area of a character is changed in the ciphertext. How about we talk about some significant symmetric figures.

DES (Data Encryption Standard) - DES is a symmetric-key square figure structured by IBM. A square figure partitions the plaintext into squares and uses a similar key to encode and unscramble the squares. DES encodes a 64-piece plaintext square utilizing a 64-piece key. It is broadly utilized in military, aviation and insight foundations in light of its quick activity and security.

Triple DES - It is progressed from DES since three keys are utilized in progression to scramble a message. It has additionally expanded the key size to 112 bits.

AES (Advanced Encryption Standard) - AES is an exceptionally mind boggling round figure with three distinctive key sizes: 128, 192, or 156 bits.

Thought (International Data Encryption Algorithm) - It was created by Xuejia Lai and james Massey. The square size is 64 bits and key size is 128 bits.

Blowfish - It was created by Bruce Schneier. The square size is 64 and key size somewhere in the range of 32 and 448.

CAST-128 - It was created via Carlisle Adams and Stafford Tavares. The square size is 64 bits and key size is 128 bits.

RC5 - RC5 was structured by Ron Rivest. It has distinctive square size and key sizes.

Asymmetric-Key Cryptography

This uses two keys: a private key and a public key. Public key is utilized to scramble to message while private key is utilized to decode. The public encryption key is made accessible to whoever needs to utilize it, however the private key is stayed quiet by the key proprietor. The procedure is clarified underneath:

- If A needs to make an impression on B, the message is encoded by An utilizing B's public key.

- If B gets the message, the message is unscrambled by utilizing B's private key. No other beneficiary can decode the message.

RSA - It is most regularly utilized public key algorithm. It is named by its creators name Rivest, Shamir, and Adelman (RSA). It utilizes two numbers as the public and private keys. RSA is valuable for short messages and furthermore utilized in digital signatures. Be that as it may, it is moderate if the message size is long.

Chapter Two

History of Encryption and Ciphers

Conveying messages across adversary lines, setting up 12 PM meeting, or secret assaults all have been reinforced by utilizing secret codes. Ciphers and codes have been utilized since old occasions in a wide range of shapes and structures to shield messages from being caught. Ciphers and codes have even crawled into numerous famous mediums from Harry Potter books to the hit film and book, The Da Vinci Code.

Today, we despite everything see ciphers as encryption. Encryption is the capacity to render a message mixed up without unique information to decode it. It's all over, from encoded government secrets to emails sent around the workplace; the utilization of encryption has become a piece of regular daily existence.

Ciphers and Codes

In spite of the fact that ciphers and codes are frequently thought to be a similar they are, truth be told, two separate techniques for camouflaging communication data.

Codes give trades to pictures, words, or numbers for words or expresses and will just have a set measure of words or expressions that can be decoded.

Ciphers trade singular letters for different letters or numbers separating messages to a far more prominent degree.

Ciphers additionally have the upside of having the option to be moved rapidly since as opposed to having a set number of expressions or words in a code it utilizes an algorithm to characterize any conceivable word or expression.

Through the unpredictable and deliberate nature of ciphers, which are utilized over codes for encryption. By taking a gander at the historical backdrop of ciphers we can show signs of improvement comprehension of how and why encryption functions in this day and age.

Atbash - A Basic Cipher

Early religion furnished us with the absolute most essential ciphers we think about. Judaism delivered the Atbash.

Atbash is a "substitution cipher", which implies that each letter is traded for another in the letters in order. Right now, the principal letter of the letter set for the last. While this is exceptionally essential, a great many people couldn't peruse not to mention break codes at 600BC.

When in Rome, Keep Secrets: The Caesar Shift

Old Rome and popular ruler Julius Caesar conveyed ciphers to new level. Caesar utilized a cipher as a way to convey orders to his commanders and partners. Utilizing what might be later named "Caesar move", he made his messages ambiguous to the individuals who didn't have the move arrangement.

Another type of substitution cipher the strategy was to just move the letter needed by three later for instance, A > D, B >E and C >F. On the off chance that a message said "spy" would seem as though this in the Caesar Shift:

S > V, P >S and Y >B. vsb

The expression "promotion astra," go for the stars would mean "DG DVWUD" in the Caesar Shift

It was immediately adjusted to be any factor measure of spots in the move.

Rot13 - A Cipher Novelty

ROT13 seems like something Hermione Granger utilizes on her O.W.L.s.(2) , however is a variety of the Caesar Shift, it utilizes a 13 letter/character substitution arrangement. Rot13 is as yet utilized regularly today, however more as oddity than staying quiet.

Message sheets that uncover the closure of a book or film have utilized the Rot13 strategy to shield others from unintentionally understanding spoilers. Harry Potter fans, you may simply discover what "he who must not be named" signifies to do to youthful Mr. Potter in book seven, the Deathly Hallows.

Modern Encryption

The coming of the PC reformed the universe of codes. The entirety of the ciphers above could be split with PC programs surprisingly fast with the correct programming. Both the structure and breaking of more grounded ciphers have been blasting along as innovation gives new apparatuses that have perpetually changed cryptography. Modern employments of ciphers have prompted propelled PC innovation that is known as encryption.

One strategy for encryption is Public Key Encryption (PKE). The PKE cipher is profoundly more grounded than those utilized in antiquated occasions. Envision two prime numbers (a number that must be separated by one and itself) for instance 17 and 13. At the point when you increase these two numbers you think of 221, and is known as the modulus.

To a pariah, 221 would have no importance since there are a lot of components that could be separated. There likewise should be an irregular number that has a worth somewhere close to 1 and the result of the two prime numbers. In a PKE cipher, a recipe is made where the a variable will be searched out:

Prime#1 * Prime#2= A

Random# must be among 1 and A

Arrangement Must be an entire Number

(X * random#)- 1 = (Prime#1-1) * (Prime#2-1)

X will be the private key utilized for the encryption and the two prime numbers will be the public key given out. As should be obvious, if PKE is Superman, Atbash is a single adaptable cell.

To locate each number's code you would take the estimation of a number (A=1 and... Z=26) and raise it to the intensity of the irregular number utilized before. After that each number is made sense of utilizing a framework called "measured math" (3) .

On the off chance that this sounds confounding don't stress that is the purpose of cipher! The prime numbers utilized in programming encryptions are many digits long. Making it significantly increasingly secure and hard for somebody to attempt to find how the code can be broken. It would take the Bat PC, Professor Dumbledore and an army of Scooby's to break a PKE cipher.

For scrambling PC records, a similar procedure happens where the document is separated into areas of bits. The littler the quantity of bits per segment, the more grounded the degree of encryption will be. Rather than letters being changed over it is 0 and 1 of double.

Advancement of Encryption: Email Anti-Theft, Locking Down Your Email

Not just has the quality of encryption expanded significantly with PC speeds, however it has gotten utilized in ordinary activities. Email Anti-Theft programming can permit people who think nothing about encryption to apply overwhelming assurance settings to outbound email documents without hardly lifting a finger as a decoded email. Email against burglary innovation permits a framework where there's no manual key trade, yet the outbound email documents don't lose any encryption quality when sent outside your organization.

Significance of Encryption

PCs aren't the costly and slow behemoths they were during the 1970s, 1980s and 1990s. Today the even the most reasonable PC can store innumerable records and run a huge number of situations a moment. To secure private data the encryptions must be sufficiently able to suffer electronic assaults.

A feeble cipher can have its algorithm found and deciphered rapidly; where as solid encryption could withstand practically any length of deciphering ambushes. While you may not be sending orders to you armed forces in the east, your email messages, banking records and other private bits of data despite everything merit the most elevated level of security.

Advanced Encryption Standard

The more well known and generally received symmetric encryption algorithm liable to be experienced these days is the Advanced Encryption Standard (AES). It is found at any rate six time quicker than triple DES.

A swap for DES was required as its key size was excessively little. With expanding figuring power, it was viewed as defenseless against comprehensive key inquiry assault. Triple DES was intended to conquer this downside yet it was discovered moderate.

The highlights of AES are as per the following –

Symmetric key symmetric square cipher

128-piece data, 128/192/256-piece keys

More grounded and quicker than Triple-DES

Give full determination and configuration subtleties

Programming implementable in C and Java

Activity of AES

AES is an iterative instead of Feistel cipher. It depends on 'substitution–stage organize'. It includes a progression of connected tasks, some of which include supplanting contributions by explicit yields (substitutions) and others include rearranging bits around (changes).

Curiously, AES plays out the entirety of its calculations on bytes as opposed to bits. Consequently, AES treats the 128 bits of a plaintext obstruct as 16 bytes. These 16 bytes are orchestrated in four segments and four columns for preparing as a framework –

In contrast to DES, the quantity of rounds in AES is variable and relies upon the length of the key. AES utilizes 10 rounds for 128-piece keys, 12 rounds for 192-piece keys and 14 rounds for 256-piece keys. Every one of these rounds utilizes an alternate 128-piece round key, which is determined from the first AES key.

The schematic of AES structure is given in the accompanying outline –

AES Structure

Encryption Process

Here, we limit to portrayal of a normal round of AES encryption. Each round contain four sub-forms. The first round procedure is delineated beneath −

First Round Process

Byte Substitution (SubBytes)

The 16 information bytes are subbed by looking into a fixed table (S-box) given in plan. The outcome is in a grid of four lines and four segments.

Shiftrows

Every one of the four columns of the network is moved to one side. Any sections that 'tumble off' are re-embedded on the correct side of line. Move is done as follows −

First line isn't moved.

Second line is moved one (byte) position to one side.

Third column is moved two situations to one side.

Fourth column is moved three situations to one side.

The outcome is another lattice comprising of a similar 16 bytes yet moved regarding one another.

MixColumns

Every segment of four bytes is currently changed utilizing an exceptional numerical capacity. This capacity takes as info the four bytes of one section and yields four totally new bytes, which supplant the first segment. The outcome is another new framework comprising of 16 new bytes. It ought to be noticed that this progression isn't acted in the last round.

Addroundkey

The 16 bytes of the lattice are currently considered as 128 bits and are XORed to the 128 bits of the round key. On the off chance that this is the last round, at that point the yield is the ciphertext. Something else, the subsequent 128 bits are deciphered as 16 bytes and we start another comparative round.

Decryption Process

The procedure of decryption of an AES ciphertext is like the encryption procedure in the switch request. Each round comprises of the four procedures directed in the invert request –

Include round key

Blend sections

Move lines

Byte substitution

Since sub-forms in each round are backward way, not at all like for a Feistel Cipher, the encryption and decryption algorithms should be independently executed, despite the fact that they are firmly related.

AES Analysis

Right now, AES is generally embraced and bolstered in both equipment and programming. Till date, no down to earth cryptanalytic assaults against AES has been found.

Moreover, AES has worked in adaptability of key length, which permits a level of 'future-sealing' against progress in the capacity to perform comprehensive key hunts.

In any case, similarly with respect to DES, the AES security is guaranteed just on the off chance that it is accurately executed and great key management is utilized.

Traditional Ciphers

In the second chapter, we discussed the fundamentals of modern cryptography. We equated cryptography with a toolkit where various cryptographic techniques are considered as the basic tools. One of these tools is the Symmetric Key Encryption where the key used for encryption and decryption is the same.

In this chapter, we discuss this technique further and its applications to develop various cryptosystems.

Earlier Cryptographic Systems Before proceeding further, you need to know some facts about historical cryptosystems —

All of these systems are based on symmetric key encryption scheme. The only security service these systems provide is confidentiality of information.

Unlike modern systems which are digital and treat data as binary numbers, the earlier systems worked on alphabets as basic element. These earlier cryptographic systems are also referred to as Ciphers.

In general, a cipher is simply just a set of steps (an algorithm) for performing both an encryption, and the corresponding decryption.

Caesar Cipher

It is a mono-alphabetic cipher wherein each letter of the plaintext is substituted by another letter to form the ciphertext. It is a simplest form of substitution cipher scheme. This cryptosystem is generally referred to as the Shift Cipher.

The concept is to replace each alphabet by another alphabet which is 'shifted' by some fixed number between 0 and 25.

For this type of scheme, both sender and receiver agree on a 'secret shift number' for shifting the alphabet. This number which is between 0 and 25 becomes the key of encryption.

The name 'Caesar Cipher' is occasionally used to describe the Shift Cipher when the 'shift of three' is used. Process of Shift Cipher In order to encrypt a plaintext letter, the sender positions the sliding ruler underneath the first set of plaintext letters and slides it to LEFT by the number of positions of the secret shift.

The plaintext letter is then encrypted to the ciphertext letter on the sliding ruler underneath. The result of this process is depicted in the following illustration for an agreed shift of three positions. In this case, the plaintext 'tutorial' is encrypted to the ciphertext `WXWRULDO'. Here is the ciphertext alphabet for a Shift of 3 —

Process of Shift Cipher

On receiving the ciphertext, the receiver who also knows the secret shift, positions his sliding ruler underneath the ciphertext alphabet and slides it to RIGHT by the agreed shift number, 3 in this case.

He then replaces the ciphertext letter by the plaintext letter on the sliding ruler underneath. Hence the ciphertext `WXWRULDO' is decrypted to 'tutorial'. To decrypt a message encoded with a Shift of 3, generate the plaintext alphabet using a shift of `-3' as shown below —

Process of Shift Cipher Security Value

Caesar Cipher is not a secure cryptosystem because there are only 26 possible keys to try out. An attacker can carry out an exhaustive key search with available limited computing resources.

Simple Substitution Cipher

It is an improvement to the Caesar Cipher. Instead of shifting the alphabets by some number, this scheme uses some permutation of the letters in alphabet. For example, A.B.....Y.Z and Z Y B.A are two obvious permutation of all the letters in alphabet. Permutation is nothing but a jumbled up set of alphabets. With 26 letters in alphabet, the possible permutations are 26! (Factorial of 26) which is equal to 4x1026. The sender and the receiver may choose any one of these possible permutation as a ciphertext alphabet. This permutation is the secret key of the scheme.

Process of Simple Substitution Cipher

Write the alphabets A, B, C,...,Z in the natural order.

The sender and the receiver decide on a randomly selected permutation of the letters of the alphabet. Underneath the natural order alphabets, write out the chosen permutation of the letters of the alphabet. For encryption, sender replaces each plaintext letters by substituting the permutation letter that is directly beneath it in the table. This process is shown in the following illustration. In this example, the chosen permutation is K,D, G, O. The plaintext 'point' is encrypted to `MJBXZ'.

Here is a jumbled Ciphertext alphabet, where the order of the ciphertext letters is a key.

Simple Substitution Cipher

On receiving the ciphertext, the receiver, who also knows the randomly chosen permutation, replaces each ciphertext letter on the bottom row with the corresponding plaintext letter in the top row. The ciphertext `MJBXZ' is decrypted to 'point'.

Security Value

Simple Substitution Cipher is a considerable improvement over the Caesar Cipher. The possible number of keys is large (26!) and even the modern computing systems are not yet powerful enough to comfortably launch a brute force attack to break the system. However, the Simple Substitution Cipher has a simple design and it is prone to design flaws, say choosing obvious permutation, this cryptosystem can be easily broken.

Monoalphabetic and Polyalphabetic Cipher

Monoalphabetic cipher is a substitution cipher in which for a given key, the cipher alphabet for each plain alphabet is fixed throughout the encryption process. For example, if 'A' is encrypted as `D', for any number of occurrence in that plaintext, 'A' will always get encrypted to `D'.

All of the substitution ciphers we have discussed earlier in this chapter are monoalphabetic; these ciphers are highly susceptible to cryptanalysis.

Polyalphabetic Cipher is a substitution cipher in which the cipher alphabet for the plain alphabet may be different at different places during the encryption process. The next two examples, playfair and Vigenere Cipher are polyalphabetic ciphers.

Playfair Cipher

In this scheme, pairs of letters are encrypted, instead of single letters as in the case of simple substitution cipher.

In playfair cipher, initially a key table is created. The key table is a 5X5 grid of alphabets that acts as the key for encrypting the plaintext. Each of the 25 alphabets must be unique and one letter of the alphabet (usually J) is omitted from the table as we need only 25 alphabets instead of 26. If the plaintext contains J, then it is replaced by I.

The sender and the receiver deicide on a particular key, say 'tutorials'. In a key table, the first characters (going left to right) in the table is the phrase, excluding the duplicate letters. The rest of the table will be filled with the remaining letters of the alphabet, in natural order. The key table works out to be —

Process of Playfair Cipher

First, a plaintext message is split into pairs of two letters (digraphs). If there is an odd number of letters, a Z is added to the last letter. Let us say we want to encrypt the message "hide money". It will be written as

HI DE MO NE YZ The rules of encryption are —

If both the letters are in the same column, take the letter below each one (going back to the top if at the bottom)

If both letters are in the same row, take the letter to the right of each one (going back to the left if at the farthest right) If neither of the preceding two rules are true, form a rectangle with the two letters and take the letters on the horizontal opposite corner of the rectangle.

Using these rules, the result of the encryption of 'hide money' with the key of 'tutorials' would be —

QC EF NU MF ZV

Decrypting the Playfair cipher is as simple as doing the same process in reverse. Receiver has the same key and can create the same key table, and then decrypt any messages made using that key.

Security Value

It is also a substitution cipher and is difficult to break compared to the simple substitution cipher. As in case of substitution cipher, cryptanalysis is possible on the Playfair cipher as well, however it would be against 625 possible pairs of letters (25x25 alphabets) instead of 26 different possible alphabets.

The Playfair cipher was used mainly to protect important, yet non-critical secrets, as it is quick to use and requires no special equipment.

Vigenere Cipher

This scheme of cipher uses a text string (say, a word) as a key, which is then used for doing a number of shifts on the plaintext. For example, let's assume the key is 'point'. Each alphabet of the key is converted to its respective numeric value: In this case, p —> 16, o —> 15, i —> 9, n —> 14, and t —> 20. Thus, the key is: 16 15 9 14 20. Process of Vigenere Cipher

The sender and the receiver decide on a key. Say 'point' is the key. Numeric representation of this key is `16 15 9 14 20'.

The sender wants to encrypt the message, say 'attack from south east'. He will arrange plaintext and numeric key as follows —

He now shifts each plaintext alphabet by the number written below it to create ciphertext as shown below

Create Ciphertext Here, each plaintext character has been shifted by a different amount — and that amount is determined by the key. The key must be less than or equal to the size of the message.

For decryption, the receiver uses the same key and shifts received ciphertext in reverse order to obtain the plaintext.

Ciphertext in Reverse Order Security Value Vigenere Cipher was designed by tweaking the standard Caesar cipher to reduce the effectiveness of cryptanalysis on the ciphertext and make a cryptosystem more robust. It is significantly more secure than a regular Caesar Cipher. In the history, it was regularly used for protecting sensitive political and military information. It was referred to as the unbreakable cipher due to the difficulty it posed to the cryptanalysis.

Variants of Vigenere Cipher

There are two special cases of Vigenere cipher —

The keyword length is same as plaintect message. This case is called Vernam Cipher. It is more secure than typical Vigenere cipher.

Vigenere cipher becomes a cryptosystem with perfect secrecy, which is called One-time pad. One-Time Pad The circumstances are —

The length of the keyword is same as the length of the plaintext. The keyword is a randomly generated string of alphabets. The keyword is used only once. Security Value Let us compare Shift cipher with one-time pad. Shift Cipher - Easy to Break

In case of Shift cipher, the entire message could have had a shift between 1 and 25. This is a very small size, and very easy to brute force. However, with each character now having its own individual shift between 1 and 26, the possible keys grow exponentially for the message.

One-time Pad — Impossible to Break

Let us say, we encrypt the name "point" with a one-time pad. It is a 5 letter text. To break the ciphertext by brute force, you need to try all possibilities of keys and conduct computation for (26 x 26 x 26 x 26 x 26) = 265 = 11881376 times. That's for a message with 5 alphabets. Thus, for a longer message, the computation grows exponentially with every additional alphabet. This makes it computationally impossible to break the ciphertext by brute force.

Transposition Cipher It is another type of cipher where the order of the alphabets in the plaintext is rearranged to create the ciphertext. The actual plaintext alphabets are not replaced.

An example is a 'simple columnar transposition' cipher where the plaintext is written horizontally with a certain alphabet width. Then the ciphertext is read vertically as shown. For example, the plaintext is "golden statue is in eleventh cave" and the secret random key chosen is "five". We arrange this text horizontally in table with number of column equal to key value.

Ciphers from the Classical Era

The old-style algorithms are those imagined pre-PC up until around the 1950's. The rundown beneath is generally requested by intricacy, least complex at the top.

Old style ciphers are cryptographic algorithms that have been utilized before (pre WWII). Some of them have just at any point been utilized by beginners (for example Bifid), while some of them have been utilized by armed forces to make sure about their top level communications (for example ADFGVX).

None of these algorithms are secure the extent that ensuring data goes (with today PCs to break them), so if genuine data security is required you ought to presumably take a gander with modern algorithms.

Atbash Cipher

The Atbash cipher is a substitution cipher with a particular key where the letters of the letter set are switched. For example, all as are supplanted with Zs, all Bs are supplanted with Ys, etc.

ROT13 Cipher

The ROT13 cipher isn't generally a cipher, all the more only an approach to darken data incidentally. It is frequently used to stow away for example film spoilers.

Caesar Cipher

The caesar cipher (a.k.the move cipher, Caesar's Code or Caesar Shift) is one of the soonest known and least difficult ciphers.

Relative Cipher

A kind of basic substitution cipher, exceptionally simple to split.

Rail-fence Cipher

A basic transposition cipher.

Baconian Cipher

The Baconian cipher is a 'biliteral' cipher, for example it utilizes just 2 characters. It is a substitution cipher.

Polybius Square Cipher

The Polybius Square is basically indistinguishable from the basic substitution cipher, then again, actually each plaintext character is enciphered as 2 ciphertext characters.

Straightforward Substitution Cipher

A basic cipher utilized by governments for a long time. Code is accommodated encryption, decryption and cryptanalysis.

Codes and Nomenclators Cipher

Nomenclators are a blend between substitution ciphers and Codes, utilized widely during the medieval times. Codes in different structures were spent until reasonably as of late.

Columnar Transposition Cipher

Another basic transposition cipher in which letters are organized in lines and the sections are transposed by a key.

Autokey Cipher

The Autokey cipher is firmly identified with the Vigenere cipher, it varies in how the key material is produced. The Autokey cipher utilizes a key word notwithstanding the plaintext as its key material, this makes it more secure than Vigenere.

Beaufort Cipher

Fundamentally the same as the Vigenere cipher, yet marginally extraordinary algorithm.

Porta Cipher

The Porta cipher is a polyalphabetic substitution cipher that utilizes a keyword to pick which letter set to encipher letters.

Running Key Cipher

The Running Key cipher is like the Vigenere cipher, yet the key is generally a long bit of non-rehashing content. This makes it harder to break all in all than the Vigenere or Autokey ciphers.

Vigenère and Gronsfeld Cipher

An increasingly unpredictable polyalphabetic substitution cipher. Code is accommodated encryption, decryption and cryptanalysis.

Homophonic Substitution Cipher

The Homophonic Substitution cipher is a substitution cipher in which single plaintext letters can be supplanted by any of a few diverse ciphertext letters. They are commonly significantly more hard to break than standard substitution ciphers.

Four-Square Cipher

An algorithm concocted by Felix Delastelle, distributed in 1902

Slope Cipher

An algorithm dependent on lattice hypothesis. Awesome at dissemination.

Playfair Cipher

The method encodes sets of letters (digraphs), rather than single letters as in the basic substitution cipher. The Playfair cipher is along these lines essentially harder to break since the recurrence examination utilized for straightforward substitution ciphers doesn't work with it.

ADFGVX Cipher

A fractionating transposition cipher. Utilized by the Germans during the primary universal war, however broke by the French. A significant troublesome cipher to break.

ADFGX Cipher

A fractionating transposition cipher. Utilized by the Germans during the primary universal war, firmly identified with ADFGVX (Note the additional V in the name).

Bifid Cipher

A fractionating transposition cipher. Just at any point utilized by novice cryptographers. Can be broken decently no problem at all.

Straddle Checkerboard Cipher

A substitution cipher with variable length substitutions.

Trifid Cipher

A fractionating transposition cipher. A variation of Bifid.

Base64 Cipher

Base64 isn't generally a cipher, however I see it utilized constantly for "enciphering" content, so it gets a privileged notice.

Fractionated Morse Cipher

Fractionated Morse first proselytes the plaintext to morse code, at that point enciphers fixed size squares of morse code back to letters. This strategy implies plaintext letters are blended into the ciphertext letters for example one plaintext letter doesn't guide to one ciphertext letter.

Chapter Three

Caesar Cipher in Cryptography

The Caesar Cipher system is one of the soonest and least difficult strategy for encryption procedure. It's basically a sort of substitution cipher, i.e., each letter of a given book is supplanted by a letter some fixed number of positions down the letter set. For instance, with a move of 1, A would be supplanted by B, B would become C, etc. The technique is obviously named after Julius Caesar, who evidently utilized it to speak with his authorities.

In this manner to cipher a given book we need a whole number worth, known as move which demonstrates the quantity of position each letter of the content has been descended.

The encryption can be spoken to utilizing measured number-crunching by first changing the letters into numbers, as indicated by the plan, A = 0, B = 1... , Z = 25. Encryption of a letter by a move n can be portrayed scientifically as.

$E\_n(x) = (x+n) mod\ 26$

(Encryption Phase with shift n)

$D_n(x) = (x-n) \mod 26$

(Decryption Phase with shift n)

Examples:

Text: ABCDEFGHIJKLMNOPQRSTUVWXYZ

Shift: 23

Cipher: XYZABCDEFGHIJKLMNOPQRSTUVW

Text: ATTACKATONCE

Shift: 4

Cipher: EXXEGOEXSRGI

Algorithm for Caesar Cipher:

Input:

- A String of lower case letters, called Text.
- An Integer between 0-25 denoting the required shift.

Procedure:

- Traverse the given text one character at a time.

- For each character, transform the given character as per the rule, depending on whether we're encrypting or decrypting the text.
- Return the new string generated.

Output:

Text: ATTACKATONCE

Shift: 4

Cipher: EXXEGOEXSRGI

How to decrypt?

We can either write another function decrypt like encrypt, that'll apply the given shift in the opposite direction to decrypt the original text. However, we can use the cyclic property of the cipher under modulo, hence we can simply observe

Cipher(n) = De-cipher(26-n)

Hence, we can use the same function to decrypt, instead, we'll modify the shift value such that shift = 26-shift (Refer this for a sample run in C++).

Bifid Cipher in Cryptography

This cipher method considered increasingly secure contrasted with other substitution algorithms reason being it breaks the message separated into two separate streams and afterward recombines them. It is a blend of the Polybius square with the transposition and utilizations fractionation to accomplish dissemination. This scrambling method developed by Felin Delastelle. It simply just at any point utilized by novice cryptographers.

Encoding Algorithm:

For this cipher system algorithm, we utilize the 25-letter "key-Square" table.

Model:

1 2 3 4 5

1 R A N C H

2 O B D E F

3 G I K L M

4 P Q S T U

5 V W X Y Z

Here we blended J with the I since we are utilizing a 5 X 5 square key network, so we can utilize just 25 characters out of the 26.

Let us take "RAMSWARUP IS THE STUDENT OF THE NIT CALICUT" as our plain content.

Step-1:

Presently discover each letter of the plain content in the key-square and compose the comparing line number and section in two separate lines. For instance, our first letter is the "R" which is available in the principal line and first segment, so the key cipher content key an incentive for it is "1-1".

RAMSWARUP IS THE STUDENT OF THE NIT CALICUT

Line: 113451144 34 412 4442214 22 412 134 1133144

COL: 125322151 23 454 3453434 15 454 324 4242454

Step-2:

Presently select a specific measure of size (this is known as the period) which demonstrate what number of key qualities we are going to take. for instance right now the square size is 5. So isolate the qualities in the square of the period.

Column: 11345 11443 44124 44221 42241 21341 13314 4

COL: 12532 21512 34543 45343 41545 43244 24245 4

Step-3:

Presently consolidate the estimations of lines and sections. Lines esteems followed by the sections. Last qualities in the wake of consolidating the estimations of lines and sections:

1134512532   1144321512   4412434543   4422145343 4224141545 2134143244 1331424245 44

Step-4 (Final Step):

Presently select pair esteems from the last consolidated qualities and take relating character an incentive from the key-square lattice. (first worth shows the line number and second worth demonstrates the section esteems).

For instance, initially taken worth is 11 which shows the character "R" and afterward we took 34 which is speaking to the character "L".

Vernam Cipher in Cryptography

Vernam Cipher is a technique for encoding alphabetic content. It is essentially a sort of substitution cipher. Right now, appoint a number to each character of the Plain-Text, similar to (a = 0, b = 1, c = 2, ... z = 25).

Technique to take key:

In Vernam cipher algorithm, we take a key to encode the plain content which length ought to be equivalent to the length of the plain content.

Encryption Algorithm:

Appoint a number to each character of the plain-content and the key as indicated by sequential request.

Include both the number (Corresponding plain-content character number and Key character number).

Subtract the number from 26 on the off chance that the additional number is more prominent than 26, on the off chance that it isn't, at that point leave it.

Model:

Plain-Text: RAMSWARUPK

Key: RANCHOBABA

Presently as indicated by our encryption algorithm we allocate a number to each character of our plain-content and key.

PT: R A M S W A R U P K

NO: 17 0 12 18 22 0 17 20 15 10

KEY: R A N C H O B A B A

NO: 17 0 13 2 7 14 1 0 1 0

Presently include the quantity of Plain-Text and Key and in the wake of doing the expansion and subtraction activity (whenever required), we will get the comparing Cipher-Text character number.

CT-NO: 34 0 25 20 29 14 18 20 16 10

Right now, are two numbers which are more noteworthy than the 26 so we need to subtract 26 from them and in the wake of applying the subtraction activity the new Cipher content character numbers are:

CT-NO: 8 0 25 20 3 14 18 20 16 10

New Cipher-Text is in the wake of getting the comparing character from the number.

CIPHER-TEXT: I A Z U D O S U Q K

Note:

For the Decryption apply the simply turn around procedure of encryption.

CIPHER-TEXT: RLVFIRTIHATASUSTBCXSQECHUOLCITNGQQUT

Chapter Four

Quantum Cryptography

The vulnerability standard of quantum material science assembles the soonest establishments for quantum cryptography. With quantum PCs of future being relied upon to tackle the discrete logarithmic issue and the famously know cryptography strategies, for example, AES, RSA, DES, quantum cryptography turns into the predicted arrangement. Practically speaking, it is utilized to set up a common, secret and arbitrary arrangement of bits to impart between two frameworks suppose, Alice and Bob. This is known as Quantum Key Distribution. After this key is shared among Alice and Bob, further trade of data can occur through known cryptographic procedures.

In view of Heisenberg's Uncertainty Principle:

BB84 and variations –

A solitary photon beat is gone through a polarizer. Alice can utilize a specific polarizer to spellbind a solitary photon beat and encode double worth bits to the result of a specific kind (vertical, flat, roundabout and so on) of the polarizer. On accepting the photon shaft, Bob would figure the polarizer and Bob would thus be able to coordinate the cases with Alice and know the rightness of his suppositions. On the off chance that Eve would have been attempting to translate, at that point because of polarization by Eve's polarizer would have caused inconsistencies in coordinate instances of Bob and Alice and consequently they would think about listening in. Consequently in such a framework if Eve attempts to listen stealthily it will get into the notification of Alice and Bob.

The B92 convention has just two polarization states dissimilar to four in unique BB84.

BB84 has comparable convention SSP that utilizes 6 states to encode the bits.

SARG04 is another convention that utilizations constricted lasers and gives a superior outcome than BB84 in more than one photon frameworks.

In view of Quantum Entanglement:

E91 and Variants –

There is a solitary source that produces a couple of entrapped photons with Alice and Bob getting every molecule. Like BB84 plot Alice and Bob would trade encoded bits and match cases for every photon moved.

Yet, right now, result of aftereffects of match instances of Alice and Bob will be inverse as an outcome of Entanglement rule. Both of them will have supplement bits in bit strings deciphered. One of them would then be able to reverse bits to concur upon a key. Since Bell's Inequality ought not hold for entrapped particles along these lines this test can affirm the nonappearance of spy. Since essentially it is unimaginable to expect to have a third photon in entrapment with vitality levels adequate for non-perceptibility, along these lines this framework is completely secure.

SARG04 and SSP convention models can be reached out to Entangled particles hypothesis.

Potential Attacks In Quantum Cryptography:

Photon Number Splitting (PNS) Attack –

Since it is beyond the realm of imagination to expect to send a solitary photon in this way a heartbeat is sent. A portion of the photons from a heartbeat can be caught by Eve and in the wake of coordinating of bits by Alice and Bob, Eve can utilize the equivalent polarizer as done by Bob and in this way get the key without being identified.

Faked-State Attack –

Eve utilizes a copy of Bob's photon indicator and along these lines catches the photons planned for Bob and further passed it to Bob. Although Eve thinks about the encoded bit, Bob believes that he got it from Alice.

Key Management in Cryptography

Key Management:

In cryptography it is an extremely dreary errand to convey the public and private key among sender and collector. On the off chance that key is known to the outsider (counterfeiter/busybody) at that point the entire security instrument gets useless. In this way, there comes the need to make sure about the trading of keys.

There are 2 viewpoints for Key Management:

Dispersion of public keys.

Utilization of public-key encryption to disperse secret.

Dispersion of Public Key:

Public key can be dispersed in 4 different ways: Public declaration, Publicly accessible index, Public-key power, and Public-key testaments. These are clarified as following beneath.

Public Announcement:

Here the public key is communicated to everybody. Significant shortcoming of this strategy is fraud. Anybody can make a key professing to be another person and communicate it. Until fabrication is found can take on the appearance of asserted client.

Publicly Available Directory:

Right now, public key is put away at a public registry. Indexes are trusted here, with properties like Participant Registration, access and permit to adjust esteems whenever, contains passages like {name, public-key}.

Registries can be gotten to electronically still defenseless against fabrication or altering.

Public Key Authority:

It is like the index at the same time, improve security by fixing command over circulation of keys from catalog. It expects clients to know public key for the registry. At whatever point the keys are required, a constant access to catalog is made by the client to get any ideal public key safely.

Public Certification:

This time authority gives an endorsement (which ties personality to the public key) to permit key trade without ongoing access to the public position each time. The endorsement is went with some other data, for example, time of legitimacy, privileges of utilization and so on. The entirety of this substance is marked by the confided in Public-Key or Certificate Authority (CA) and it tends to be confirmed by anybody having the power's public-key.

How Ciphers Work

A cipher is an algorithm or set of algorithms that efficiently convert a sender's planned message content to what gives off an impression of being negligible content, which can be changed over back to the sender's unique message just by approved beneficiaries. The accompanying terms and definitions will assist you with comprehension ciphering and deciphering when all is said in done and the code behind them.

The term plaintext alludes the sender's unique message. The importance in plaintext is the thing that the sender needs to pass on to the recipient(s).

The term ciphertext alludes to plaintext whose appearance has been scrambled, or algorithmically changed. Ciphertext becomes plaintext once it has been decoded.

Numerous ciphers utilize at least one keys. A key is string of content or bits used to encode or decode data. RSA Data Security, Inc. (http://www.rsa.com/), a main encryption innovation firm, expresses that a key decides the mapping of the plaintext to the ciphertext. A key could be just about anything, for example, "cleveland," the expression "victors never quit, weaklings always lose," the parallel number

10011011, or even some wild string, for example, %_-.;,(<<*&^.)

Ciphers in which both the sender and the beneficiary utilize a similar key to encode and unscramble the message are said to be a piece of a symmetric-key cryptosystem. Ciphers in which data is scrambled and decoded with a couple of keys- - one uninhibitedly dispersed to the public, the other known uniquely to the beneficiary - are said to be a piece of a public-key cryptosystem. Ciphers right now a lopsided key cryptosystem.

There are many archived ciphers. Some go back a huge number of years, contrived by incredible pioneers or researchers of the past; others go back to just a week ago, conceived by some nerdy young person who experienced revelation subsequent to setting an individual high score on Tomb Raider. Whatever the source, ciphers fall into three general classes: disguise, transposition, and substitution.

Camouflage ciphers incorporate the plaintext inside the ciphertext. It is dependent upon the beneficiary to realize which letters or images to bar from the ciphertext so as to yield the plaintext. Here is a case of a covering cipher:

i2l32i5321k34e1245ch456oc12ol234at567e

Expel all the numbers, and you'll have I like chocolate. What about this one?

Larry even shows up energized. Nobody stresses.

The primary letter from each word uncovers the message leave now. Both are simple, undoubtedly, yet numerous individuals have made progressively cunning methods for disguising the messages. Coincidentally, this sort of cipher doesn't require ciphertext, for example, that in the above models. Consider the undetectable drying ink that children use to send secret messages. In an increasingly extraordinary model, a man named Histiaeus, during fifth century B.C., shaved the leader of a confided in slave, at that point inked the message onto his bare head. At the point when the slave's hair became back, Histiaeus sent the captive to the message's expected beneficiary, Aristagoros, who shaved the slave's head and read the message educating him to revolt.

Transposition ciphers likewise hold the characters of the plaintext inside the ciphertext. Ciphertext is made just by changing the request for the current plaintext characters. Attempt this one:

uoynosdn ep ed yx al ag eh tf oy te fa se ht

Pack those letters together, at that point switch their request. You'll get the message "the wellbeing of the world relies upon you."

Substitution ciphers supplant each character of plaintext with another character or image. Think about this:

9-15-14-12-25-20-8-9-14-11-9-14-14-21-13-2-5-18-19

In the event that you substitute each number with the related letter of the letter set, you'll uncover the expression "I just think in numbers." (For instance, "I" is the ninth letter of the letter set, "o" is the fifteenth, and so on.) Substitution ciphers can use pretty much any character set for encryption and decryption. The two ciphers right now substitution ciphers.

Symmetric Encryption Algorithms

Symmetric encryption algorithms get their name from the way that they utilize precisely the same key from the encryption and decryption process. For this procedure to work both the sender and the collector must have the equivalent mutual secret key to have the option to play out the encryption and decryption of the data they are transmitting.

Symmetric encryption is additionally normally alluded to as secret key encryption, on the grounds that for the communication among sender and collector to stay secure it is significant that the common key stay secure, as you can suppose anybody got hold of the key they would have the option to encode and decode messages.

There are many notable symmetric encryption algorithms, some are more typical than others, the more well known techniques are those which utilize greater key sizes, additionally their are three principle sorts of symmetric encryption strategies

Square ciphers

Message Authentication Codes (MAC)

Stream Ciphers

Symmetric techniques looked at awry encryption strategies are extremely quick and go through less assets on your gadgets and therefore they are utilized all the more frequently for mass encryption when you have to guarantee total security.

The fundamental downside to this technique for encryption is the underlying and constant safe appropriation of keys between your gadgets without the keys turning out to be undermined.

These days another strategy for key dissemination is utilized where a hilter kilter channel between two frameworks is made to construct a safe passage over which your common key will be traded before any significant client data is moved.

Chapter Five

Stream ciphers

A stream cipher plays out an encryption which is like the One-time Pad (OTP) encryption strategy. It delivers an enormous lump of secret, irregular looking data and joins it with the plaintext to create ciphertext. Without precisely the same data piece, the plaintext can't be revealed from the ciphertext. The arbitrary data speaks to a surge of bits which is gotten from the secret key and is regularly alluded to as keystream. A stream cipher contains some tenacious memory, called the interior cipher state, which is instated by the secret key and spreads to a successor state after every encryption step. The yield of a solid stream cipher is equivalent to (and ought to be indistinct from) a bordering bit stream created by a Pseudo Random Number Generator (PRNG).

To be increasingly exact, we install the comments made in and characterize a stream cipher as follows: an encryption work which works on individual plaintext digits (generally bits) where its inside state is introduced with the secret key preceding encryption. The keystream fluctuates, contingent upon the instated secret key and the snapshot of encryption concerning the spread of the inside state. Encryption of plaintext and decryption of ciphertext are both performed by the elite or (XOR) activity, which is signified by a ⊕ image and speaks to somewhat insightful expansion modulo two. A helpful numerical property of this administrator is that it very well may be altered. Hence, it tends to be applied for encryption just as decryption.

There are two sorts of stream ciphers, synchronous and self-synchronizing. In a synchronous stream cipher, the encryption bits are figured freely from the plaintext. Such ciphers are valuable in circumstances when a communication channel is increasingly inclined to mistake. It may happen that only one severely transmitted piece is wrongly deciphered, which anyway doesn't legitimately affect different bits that were moved in a right way. In this way, stream ciphers are helpful to encode spilling media where the speed of data-traffic is a higher priority than the fulfillment and respectability of the data. Conflictingly, a self-synchronizing stream cipher figures the successor of its inside state with a capacity over the past state and the ciphertext. The inside state redirects from its unique spread way when a transmission blunder happens. This exposition focusses itself on the most broadly utilized and best concentrated of the two, the synchronous stream ciphers.

Thusly, a general reference to a stream cipher alludes to a synchronous stream cipher.

A significant goal of a stream cipher is to evade an immediate connection between the info (secret key) and yield (keystream) of the cipher. Since the entropy of a stream cipher is restricted to the size of the interior express, the delivered keystream will in the long run recurrent itself. Note, this isn't a property of a customary One-time Pad (OTP).

Unadulterated One-time Pad encryption can give impeccable mystery when the keystream is really arbitrary and extraordinarily produced for each message that is transmitted. In such a setting, the keystream should comprise of a novel piece string that contains consistently dispersed irregular bits. Be that as it may, practically speaking it is difficult to create genuinely arbitrary data. Elective techniques, such as utilizing the total substance of an arbitrary book, radically limit the quantity of conceivable keystreams. Besides, reuse of the equivalent keystream is exceptionally unreliable. With access to past plaintext and ciphertext, an enemy would have the option to remove the keystream. On the off chance that the equivalent keystream is utilized in a subsequent transmission, the foe can utilize the recouped keystream and uncover the second plaintext. Precisely for this specific explanation, the encryption system is called One-time Pad. The keystream that speaks to the secret key should just be utilized once.

Keystream can be viewed as a special arrangement of bits which must be as long as the plaintext. Nonetheless, proceeding with conveyance of crisp keystream for long data successions is unwanted. With an expansion in electronic trans-missions of enormous transcripts in the twentieth century, the requirement for elective arrangements developed. Accordingly, a few stream cipher encryption strategies were presented. For example, during the 1930s stream ciphers were fundamentally utilized as physical rotor machines which worked for the most part mechanically. A notable case of such a rotor machine is the Enigma, A couple of decades later, the presentation of enormous scope PC systems expanded the interest for all the more hard-and programming focused stream ciphers which upheld computerized communication.

Run of the mill non-direct stream cipher framework

The cryptographic algorithm outlined installs a turning shift register, which speaks to the interior condition of the cipher. After the calculation of another keystream bit, the successor work refreshes the inside state by a direct capacity to save as a lot of entropy to the cipher. At that point, the yield part applies a non-direct channel work $f(\cdot)$ to register the following keystream bit. The keystream bits are utilized by the sender to scramble the plaintext bits by consolidating both piece strings with the selective or (XOR) activity. The subsequent ciphertext is transmitted over a shaky channel. The recipient plays out precisely the same calculations and applies another XOR activity, this time on the ciphertext bits in blend with the keystream bits. The keystream bits, effectively inserted in the ciphertext, are offset and the first plaintext is uncovered to the beneficiary.

The sender and the recipient utilize the non-direct stream cipher to process precisely the equivalent keystream. At that point, the sender consolidates the keystream with the plaintext to create the ciphertext by utilizing the XOR activity. The collector plays out a similar system on the ciphertext together with the keystream to remake and uncover the plaintext.

In many cryptosystems it is imperative to connect numerous scrambled messages in one crypto-realistic meeting, this is called tying of encryption. Stream ciphers naturally give this element since their ciphertext is created steadily. It utilizes the past inner state and a successor capacity to step forward.

Other than these authentic stream cipher plans there are a few new recommendations in the literature [4, 47, 57, 76]. In spite of their focal points in adaptability and speed, stream ciphers are as of now hardly utilized insecure frameworks that give solid cryptographic security. Run of the mill stream cipher assaults intend to isolate the plaintext from the encryption bits. For example, a pliability assault abuses a general and unavoidable shortcoming in customary stream ciphers where the keystream is produced autonomously from the plaintext. Little modifications (bit-turns) to the ciphertext may be sufficient to play out the assault without really recouping the secret key. More subtleties are given in Section.

The security that is given by the hidden structure squares of stream ciphers is very much considered. In any case, the security ramifications of these different parts may not hold when they are consolidated and utilized together in one cryptographic algorithm. Rather, the complete security ramifications of square ciphers are better comprehended [19, 25].

Cryptographic assaults

This area presents seven essential cryptanalytic methods which are utilized in cryptography assaults, additionally alluded to as cryptanalysis. There are a lot further developed and complex cryptographic assault philosophies and procedures proposed in the writing [18, 22, 24, 26, 44, 45, 54, 84, 125]. In any case, to look after lucidness, without a doubt, exceptionally simple forms of the essential procedures are presented. The sort of cryptosystem that is principally used to show the assault methods is a variation of the non-direct stream cipher framework.

To mount a cryptographic assault, it now and again requires huge computational effort to recuperate the secret key. The processing power that is required mirrors the assault multifaceted nature, see Section 1.1. It is conceivable to sum up the calculations that are required for a cryptographic assault so that they can be (halfway) pre-figured. Such method is normally alluded to as Time-Memory Trade-Off (TMTO). The general thought is to part a cryptographic assault into two stages, a pre-calculation stage (off-line) and dynamic assault stage (on-line). For more data on this subject, kindly allude to the TMTO strategies and efficient search systems proposed in the writing [2, 10–12, 20, 21, 27, 61, 77, 80, 102, 115, 117].

Malleability assault

The points of interest of a synchronous stream cipher that creates a non-straight twofold succession are clarified. It shows a representation of a common cryptosystem that utilizations such a cipher. The produced double grouping fills in as the keystream and is joined with the plaintext by applying the selective or (XOR) administrator. Such a cryptosystem could in principle give a safe channel which secures the secrecy of the data transmission. Be that as it may, moving along without any more insurance, the respectability of the data isn't ensured. Extra countermeasures, for example, a Message Authentication Code (MAC), can secure the credibility of the data. Without strengthening cryptographic methods a stream cipher framework is defenceless against a pliability assault.

During a pliability assault, the ciphertext is changed so that it despite everything decodes to genuine plaintext, yet fulfils the assailant's motivation. Note, that the objective of a pliability assault isn't to recoup the secret key. Actually, it attempts to undermine the security of the cryptosystem without having any information on the secret key. Figure 2.1 exhibits a data transmission altering of a financial application that is helpless against a pliability assault. A genuinely little cash move is adjusted by a solitary piece flip and unexpectedly speaks to an extremely huge cash move. Regardless of whether the keystream is created by an incredibly secure stream cipher, different segments of the cryptosystem may, in any case, be powerless. It is the quality of the whole cryptosystem that characterizes the real security.

Albeit a pliability assault gives off an impression of being incredible, it isn't that clear to mount. The foe has to know precisely where and when the sum is transmitted to have the option to mess with it. Somewhat flip at an erroneous position is negligible and will in all probability bring about an undermined transmission. Information about the keystream permits a foe to get ready all the more deliberately created altering. In any case, this includes reuse of the keystream, a circumstance which a stream cipher ought to dodge no matter what. As Section 1.2 states, it is significant that the twofold arrangement is utilized just a single time. To implement this, the interior state ought to be introduced with a one of a kind worth each time the stream cipher is utilized. For example, such a worth can be gotten from a secret key in mix with crisp irregular difficulties.

A safe trade of new irregular difficulties and an ensured Initialization Vector (IV) of the cipher is definitely not a trifling assignment. Truth be told, a few restrictive stream ciphers permit a foe to impact the instatement of the inward state so that precisely the equivalent keystream is delivered as it was produced in a past meeting. A complete, yet useful, case of a stream cipher flexibility assault is given in [48]. It depicts the main viable assault on the MIFARE cryptosystem. The memory substance of a MIFARE Classic smartcard can be uncovered even with no information on the secret key. The MIFARE cryptosystem is additionally examined and various assaults showed up in the writing [34, 37, 41, 62, 62, 64, 67, 81, 95, 100, 101, 118, 119, 121, 122, 126].

Hash Function

What is a Hash Function?

A capacity that changes over a given huge telephone number to a little down to earth whole number worth. The mapped whole number worth is utilized as a record in the hash table. In straightforward terms, a hash work maps a major number or string to a little whole number that can be utilized as the list in the hash table.

What is implied by Good Hash Function?

A decent hash capacity ought to have the accompanying properties:

Proficiently processable.

Ought to consistently disseminate the keys (Each table position similarly likely for each key)

For instance: For telephone numbers, an awful hash work is to take the initial three digits. A superior capacity is viewed as the last three digits. It would be ideal if you note this may not be the best hash work. There might be better ways.

By and by, we can regularly utilize heuristic procedures to make a hash work that performs well. Subjective data about the conveyance of the keys might be helpful right now. All in all, a hash capacity ought to rely upon each and every piece of the key, with the goal that two keys that vary in just the slightest bit or one gathering of bits (whether or not the gathering is toward the start, end, or center of the key or present all through the key) hash into various qualities. Along these lines, a hash work that basically extricates a segment of a key isn't appropriate. Essentially, if two keys are just digited or character changes of one another, (for example, 139 and 319), they ought to likewise hash into various qualities.

The two heuristic strategies are hashing by division and hashing by duplication which are as per the following:

The mod strategy:

Right now making hash capacities, we map a key into one of the spaces of table by taking the rest of key partitioned by table_size. That is, the hash work is

h(key) = key mod table_size

for example key % table_size

Since it requires just a solitary division activity, hashing by division is very quick.

When utilizing the division technique, we for the most part maintain a strategic distance from specific estimations of table_size like table_size ought not be an intensity of a number guess r, since on the off chance that table_size = r^p, at that point h(key) is only the p least request bits of key. Except if we realize that all low-request p-bit designs are similarly likely, we are in an ideal situation planning the hash capacity to rely upon all the bits of the key.

It has been discovered that the best outcomes with the division technique are accomplished when the table size is prime. Be that as it may, regardless of whether table_size is prime, an extra limitation is called for. On the off chance that r is the quantity of conceivable character codes on a PC, and on the off chance that table_size is a prime to such an extent that r % table_size equivalent 1, at that point hash work h(key) = key % table_size is just the whole of the double portrayal of the characters in the key mod table_size.

Model:

Assume r = 256 and table_size = 17, in which r % table_size for example 256 % 17 = 1.

So for key = 37596, its hash is

37596 % 17 = 12

Be that as it may, for key = 573, its hash work is moreover

573 % 12 = 12

Subsequently it tends to be seen that by this hash work, numerous keys can have a similar hash. This is called Collision.

A prime not very near an accurate intensity of 2 is regularly acceptable decision for table_size.

The increase technique:

In increase technique, we duplicate the key k by a consistent genuine number c in the range 0 < c < 1 and concentrate the partial piece of k * c.

At that point we duplicate this incentive by table_size m and take the floor of the outcome. It very well may be spoken to as

h(k) = floor (m * (k * c mod 1))

or on the other hand

h(k) = floor (m * frac (k * c))

where the capacity floor(x), accessible in standard library math.h, yields the whole number piece of the genuine number x, and frac(x) yields the fragmentary part. [frac(x) = x − floor(x)]

A favorable position of the duplication technique is that the estimation of m isn't basic, we normally pick it to be an intensity of 2 (m = 2p for some whole number p), since we can then effectively execute the capacity on most PCs

Assume that the word size of the machine is w bits and that key fits into a solitary word.

We limit c to be a small amount of the structure s/(2w), where s is a number in the range 0 < s < 2w.

Alluding to figure, we initially increase key by the w-bit number s = c * 2w. The outcome is a 2w-bit esteem

r1 * 2w + r0

where r1 = high-request expression of the item

r0 = lower request expression of the item

Despite the fact that this technique works with any estimation of the steady c, it works preferable with certain qualities over the others.

c ~ (sqrt (5) − 1)/2 = 0.618033988 . . .

is probably going to work sensibly well.

Model:

Assume k = 123456, p = 14,

m = 2^14 = 16384, and w = 32.

Adjusting Knuth's recommendation, c to be division of the structure s/2^32.

At that point key * s = 327706022297664 = (76300 * 2^32) + 17612864,

So r1 = 76300 and r0 = 176122864.

The 14 most noteworthy bits of r0 yield the worth h(key) = 67.

Highlights of Hash Functions

The run of the mill highlights of hash capacities are −

Fixed Length Output (Hash Value)

Hash work coverts data of self-assertive length to a fixed length. This procedure is regularly alluded to as hashing the data.

As a rule, the hash is a lot littler than the info data, thus hash capacities are once in a while called pressure capacities.

Since a hash is a littler portrayal of a bigger data, it is likewise alluded to as an overview.

Hash work with n bit yield is alluded to as a n-bit hash work. Mainstream hash capacities create values somewhere in the range of 160 and 512 bits.

Productivity of Operation

For the most part for any hash work h with input x, calculation of h(x) is a quick activity.

Computationally hash capacities are a lot quicker than a symmetric encryption.

Properties of Hash Functions

So as to be a powerful cryptographic device, the hash work is wanted to have following properties –

Pre-Image Resistance

This property implies that it ought to be computationally difficult to turn around a hash work.

As it were, on the off chance that a hash work h created a hash esteem z, at that point it ought to be a troublesome procedure to discover any info esteem x that hashes to z.

This property ensures against an assailant who just has a hash esteem and is attempting to discover the info.

Second Pre-Image Resistance

This property implies given an information and its hash, it ought to be elusive an alternate contribution with a similar hash.

At the end of the day, if a hash work h for an info x produces hash esteem h(x), at that point it ought to be hard to locate some other information esteem y with the end goal that h(y) = h(x).

This property of hash work ensures against an aggressor who has an information worth and its hash, and needs to substitute distinctive incentive as real incentive instead of unique info esteem.

Collision Resistance

This property implies it ought to be elusive two distinct contributions of any length that bring about a similar hash. This property is additionally alluded to as impact free hash work.

At the end of the day, for a hash work h, it is elusive any two distinct sources of info x and y with the end goal that h(x) = h(y).

Since, hash work is compacting capacity with fixed hash length, it is unthinkable for a hash work not to have impacts. This property of impact free just affirms that these crashes ought to be elusive.

This property makes it hard for an assailant to discover two information esteems with a similar hash.

Likewise, in the event that a hash work is crash safe, at that point it is second pre-picture safe.

Well known Hash Functions

Let us quickly observe some famous hash capacities –

Message Digest (MD)

MD5 was generally well known and broadly utilized hash work for very a few years.

The MD family involves hash capacities MD2, MD4, MD5 and MD6. It was embraced as Internet Standard RFC 1321. It is a 128-piece hash work.

MD5 digests have been generally utilized in the product world to give confirmation about trustworthiness of moved document. For instance, record servers frequently give a pre-registered MD5 checksum for the documents, with the goal that a client can look at the checksum of the downloaded document to it.

In 2004, crashes were found in MD5. An explanatory assault was accounted for to be fruitful just in an hour by utilizing PC bunch. This impact assault came about in undermined MD5 and thus it is never again prescribed for use.

Secure Hash Function (SHA)

Group of SHA include four SHA algorithms; SHA-0, SHA-1, SHA-2, and SHA-3. Despite the fact that from same family, there are basically extraordinary.

The first form is SHA-0, a 160-piece hash work, was distributed by the National Institute of Standards and Technology (NIST) in 1993. It had scarcely any shortcomings and didn't turn out to be famous. Later in 1995, SHA-1 was intended to address affirmed shortcomings of SHA-0.

SHA-1 is the most generally utilized of the current SHA hash capacities. It is utilized in a few broadly utilized applications and protocols including Secure Socket Layer (SSL) security.

In 2005, a technique was found for revealing impacts for SHA-1 inside pragmatic time span making long haul employability of SHA-1 dubious.

SHA-2 family has four further SHA variations, SHA-224, SHA-256, SHA-384, and SHA-512 relying up upon number of bits in their hash esteem. No fruitful assaults have yet been accounted for on SHA-2 hash work.

In spite of the fact that SHA-2 is a solid hash work. Despite the fact that fundamentally unique, its essential structure is still follows plan of SHA-1. Henceforth, NIST called for new serious hash work structures.

In October 2012, the NIST picked the Keccak algorithm as the new SHA-3 standard. Keccak offers numerous advantages, for example, productive execution and great obstruction for assaults.

RIPEMD

The RIPEND is an abbreviation for RACE Integrity Primitives Evaluation Message Digest. This arrangement of hash capacities was structured by open research network and by and large known as a group of European hash capacities.

The set incorporates RIPEND, RIPEMD-128, and RIPEMD-160. There likewise exist 256, and 320-piece adaptations of this algorithm.

Unique RIPEMD (128 piece) depends on the plan standards utilized in MD4 and found to give sketchy security. RIPEMD 128-piece adaptation came as a convenient solution substitution to conquer vulnerabilities on the first RIPEMD.

RIPEMD-160 is an improved adaptation and the most generally utilized form in the family. The 256 and 320-piece renditions diminish the opportunity of inadvertent impact, yet don't have more elevated levels of security when contrasted with RIPEMD-128 and RIPEMD-160 individually.

Whirlpool

This is a 512-piece hash work.

It is gotten from the changed variant of Advanced Encryption Standard (AES). One of the originator was Vincent Rijmen, a co-maker of the AES.

Three variants of Whirlpool have been discharged; to be specific WHIRLPOOL-0, WHIRLPOOL-T, and WHIRLPOOL.

Digital Signatures

Since we comprehend what hashes are, we can clarify how they are utilized in SSL Certificates.

The SSL/TLS convention is utilized to empower secure transmission of data starting with one gadget then onto the next over the web. For conciseness, it appears SSL is regularly clarified as "encryption." But remember that SSL likewise gives authentication. The SSL testament document is entrusted with giving the important data expected to authentication. Or on the other hand put another way, SSL endorsements tie a particular public key to a character.

Recollect that the SSL/TLS convention encourages an association utilizing deviated encryption. This implies there are two encryption keys that each handle one portion of the procedure: a public key for encryption, and a private key for decryption. Each SSL endorsement contains a public key that can be utilized by the customer to encode data, and the proprietor of said SSL testament safely stores a private key on their server which they use to unscramble that data and make it lucid.

At last, the basic role of this uneven encryption is secure key trade. Attributable to the processing power hilter kilter keys require, it's increasingly pragmatic (and still sheltered) to utilize littler symmetric keys for the real communication segment of the association. So the customer produces a meeting key, at that point encodes a duplicate of it and sends it to the server where it very well may be unscrambled and utilized for imparting all through the length of the association (or until it's turned out).

The is the reason Authentication is unbelievably essential to ensuring SSL/TLS really gives significant security. Envision if your PC had no dependable method to realize who possessed the encryption key you were utilizing? Scrambling your meeting key with that public key would not be valuable since you would not realize who had the relating private key that unscrambles it. All things considered, encoding data is of little use on the off chance that you are sending it straightforwardly to a man-in-the-center aggressor or a pernicious gathering at the opposite finish of the association.

Digital signatures are a significant piece of how SSL endorsements give authentication. At the point when a declaration is given, it is digitally marked by the Certificate Authority (CA) you have picked as your authentication supplier (for instance Sectigo, DigiCert, and so on). This mark gives cryptographic evidence that the CA marked the

SSL endorsement and that the authentication has not been adjusted or recreated. All the more significantly, it a genuine mark is cryptographic evidence that the data contained in the endorsement has been confirmed by a confided in outsider.

Presently we should discuss how a digital mark is made, applied, joined – you pick the wording. The hilter kilter keys we referenced before are utilized once more, however to sign not encoding. Scientifically, marking includes flipping around the manner in which the data and keys are joined (We won't go excessively far into the weeds on the points of interest of how signatures are made on the grounds that it gets muddled rapidly. In the event that you are keen on that, Joshua Davies has composed an extraordinary post on how digital signatures work). To make it simpler for PCs to rapidly, yet still safely, make and check these signatures, the CA first hashes the authentication record and signs the subsequent hash. This is more proficient than marking the whole endorsement.

That Digital signatures at that point gives the required verification that the authentication you have been given is the specific endorsement gave by a confided in CA to the site being referred to. No stunts. No mocking. No man-in-the-center control of the SSL/TLS endorsement record.

Digital signatures are amazingly delicate – any change to the document will make the mark change. On the off chance that we took our model sentence from the past area and made it altogether lowercase ("the speedy dark colored fox bounces over the apathetic canine") the subsequent hash would be completely extraordinary. That implies the subsequent mark of that hash would likewise be extraordinary. In any event, transforming the slightest bit of a multi-thousand gigabyte archive would bring about a totally extraordinary hash.

This makes it incomprehensible for an assailant to change a real authentication or make a deceitful testament that looks real. An alternate hash implies that the mark would never again be substantial, and your PC would realize this when it's confirming the SSL declaration. In the event that your PC experienced an invalid mark, it would trigger a blunder and altogether forestall a protected association.

SHA-1 and SHA-2

pki endorsement management botch, algorithms, sha, sha-2, sha-256

Since we have established the framework, we can jump on to the superstar.

As I said before, SHA represents Secure Hashing Algorithm. SHA-1 and SHA-2 are two distinct adaptations of that algorithm. They contrast in both development (how the subsequent hash is made from the first data) and in the bit-length of the mark. You should consider SHA-2 as the successor to SHA-1, as it is a general improvement.

Principally, individuals center around the bit-length as the significant qualification. SHA-1 is a 160-piece hash. SHA-2 is really a "family" of hashes and arrives in an assortment of lengths, the most famous being 256-piece.

The assortment of SHA-2 hashes can prompt a touch of disarray, as sites and creators express them in an unexpected way. In the event that you see "SHA-2," "SHA-256" or "SHA-256 piece," those names are alluding to something very similar. On the off chance that you see "SHA-224," "SHA-384," or "SHA-512," those are alluding to the other piece lengths of SHA-2. You may likewise observe a few locales being increasingly express and working out both the algorithm and bit-length, for example, "SHA-2 384." But that is disagreeable like causing individuals to incorporate your center starting when you state your name.

The SSL business has picked SHA as its hashing algorithm for digital signatures

From 2011 to 2015, SHA-1 was the essential algorithm. A developing group of research demonstrating the shortcomings of SHA-1 provoked a revaluation. Truth be told, Google has even ventured to such an extreme as to make a SHA-1 impact (when two bits of dissimilar data make a similar hash esteem) just to give. Along these lines, from 2016 ahead, SHA-2 is the new standard. On the off chance that you are accepting a SSL/TLS endorsement today it must utilize that signature at any rate.

Once in a while you will see endorsements utilizing SHA-2 384-piece. You will once in a while observe the 224-piece assortment, which isn't affirmed for use with publicly confided in testaments, or the 512-piece assortment which is less generally bolstered by programming.

SHA-2 will probably stay being used for in any event five years. In any case, some startling assault against the algorithm could be found which would incite a prior change.

Here is the thing that A SHA-1 and SHA-2 hash of our site's SSL Certificate resembles:

SHA-1, SHA-2

In this way, yes. This is the thing that all the object is about. It may not look like a lot – yet digital signatures are inconceivably significant for guaranteeing the security of SSL/TLS.

A bigger piece hash can give greater security on the grounds that there are increasingly potential mixes. Recollect that one of the significant elements of a cryptographic hashing algorithm is that is produces novel hashes. Once more, if two distinct qualities or records can deliver a similar hash, you make what we call an impact.

The security of digital signatures must be ensured as long as impacts don't happen. Impacts are incredibly hazardous in light of the fact that they permit two documents to deliver a similar mark, consequently, when a PC checks the mark, it might have all the earmarks of being legitimate despite the fact that that record was rarely really marked.

How Many Hashes?

On the off chance that a hashing algorithm should create interesting hashes for each conceivable info, exactly what number of potential hashes are there?

A piece has two potential qualities: 0 and 1. The conceivable number of extraordinary hashes can be communicated as the quantity of potential qualities raised to the quantity of bits. For SHA-256 there are 2256 potential blends.

In this way, 2256 blends. What number of is that? All things considered, it's an enormous number. Truly. It puts numbers like trillion and septillion to disgrace. It far surpasses the what number of grains of sand are on the planet.

The bigger the quantity of potential hashes, the littler the possibility that two qualities will make a similar hash.

There are (in fact) an endless number of conceivable inputs[1], yet a set number of yields. Along these lines, in the long run, each hashing algorithm, including a protected one, delivers an impact. In any case, we are for the most part worried about how simple it is do as such. SHA-1 was esteemed shaky in light of the fact that, because of the two its size and development, it was possible to create an impact.

Note that an enormous piece length doesn't consequently mean a hashing algorithm creates increasingly secure hashes. The development of the algorithm is likewise extraordinarily significant — that is the reason the SSL business utilizes hashing algorithms explicitly intended for cryptographic security.

The Move To SHA-2

In 2015 the SSL business experienced the "SHA-2 Transition." It included re-giving a huge number of existing declarations so new records could be made and marked with SHA-2. It likewise included significant updates to the issuance programming that publicly-believed CAs work (there are many them). True to form, there were a few hiccups.

The cutoff time for giving new SSL authentications with SHA-1 hashes was December 31st, 2015. Generally, the industry has stayed by that cutoff time. From that point forward, a couple of slip-ups have been made, and a couple of exceptional cases were conceded.

Be that as it may, in the course of the most recent three years SHA-1 declarations have for the most part ceased to exist. Today, in the event that you experience a SHA-1 declaration, you will see an indisputable admonition. It's been heightening. In Google Chrome, all SHA-1 declarations terminating in 2016 didn't show the green latch in secure associations, and rather showed a similar symbol as an unbound HTTP association. You can tap the symbol to get progressively explicit data concerning why it's being shown, on the off chance that there are different reasons inconsequential to the mark.

SHA-1

In the event that you saw a SHA-1 declaration in your program today, here is what it would resemble (in Google Chrome). To perceive how this page glances in your program, visit https://sha1-2016.badssl.com

Programs treated SHA-1 marked testaments that lapse in 2017 with a progressively extreme admonition. This is on the grounds that the security of a mark is legitimately identified with to what extent it's substantial.

Presently, in 2018, Google just summarily executes the site proprietor and leaves his carcass showed as a notice to others that may set out to submit similar sins.

Keeping Signatures Secure

As time advances, assaults against cryptography will improve, and PC preparing force will get less expensive. This makes a legitimate SHA-2 mark less secure in 2020 than it was in 2016. Thus, the decision of algorithm will be a lot beefier than promptly important with the goal that transient enhancements don't bring about a trade off of security. It isn't unreasonable for a specific hashing algorithm to stay secure for 10 years.

Industry specialists and security scientists over the world are constantly examining SHA-2 and other cryptographic hashing algorithms, so have confidence that current SSL authentications will have solid and secure digital signatures for some time.

That doesn't imply that cryptographers will simply lounge around and hold up until there is an issue. The successor to SHA-2, helpfully named SHA-3, has just been finished. At the point when it's an ideal opportunity to do another switch, the SSL business may utilize SHA-3 as its next decision, or it might look to an altogether changed algorithm.

Chapter Six

Message Authentication Code (MAC)

Macintosh algorithm is a symmetric key cryptographic procedure to give message authentication. For setting up MAC process, the sender and collector share a symmetric key K.

Basically, a MAC is an encoded checksum produced on the hidden message that is sent alongside a message to guarantee message authentication.

The way toward utilizing MAC for authentication is delineated in the accompanying representation –

Macintosh

Let us currently attempt to comprehend the whole procedure in detail –

The sender utilizes some publicly known MAC algorithm, inputs the message and the secret key K and produces a MAC esteem.

Like hash, MAC work additionally packs a subjective since quite a while ago contribution to a fixed length yield. The significant contrast among hash and MAC is that MAC utilizes secret key during the pressure.

The sender advances the message alongside the MAC. Here, we expect that the message is sent free, as we are worried of giving message cause authentication, not classification. In the event that classification is required, at that point the message needs encryption.

On receipt of the message and the MAC, the collector takes care of the got message and the common secret key K into the MAC algorithm and re-processes the MAC esteem.

The collector currently checks balance of crisply processed MAC with the MAC got from the sender. In the event that they coordinate, at that point the beneficiary acknowledges the message and guarantees himself that the message has been sent by the planned sender.

In the event that the registered MAC doesn't coordinate the MAC sent by the sender, the recipient can't decide if the message has been modified or the birthplace has been distorted. As a primary concern, a collector securely expect that the message isn't the veritable.

Impediments of MAC

There are two significant impediments of MAC, both because of its symmetric nature of activity –

Foundation of Shared Secret.

It can give message authentication among pre-chosen real clients who have shared key.

This requires foundation of shared secret before utilization of MAC.

Failure to Provide Non-Repudiation

Non-denial is the affirmation that a message originator can't deny any recently sent messages and duties or activities.

Macintosh strategy doesn't give a non-renouncement administration. In the event that the sender and collector engage in a disagreement about message start, MACs can't give a proof that a message was in reality sent by the sender.

In spite of the fact that no outsider can process the MAC, still sender could deny having sent the message and guarantee that the collector produced it, as it is difficult to figure out which of the two gatherings registered the MAC.

Cryptography Digital signatures

Digital signatures are the public-key natives of message authentication. In the physical world, it is entirely expected to utilize manually written signatures on transcribed or composed messages. They are utilized to tie signatory to the message.

So also, a digital mark is a system that ties an individual/element to the digital data. This coupling can be autonomously confirmed by recipient just as any outsider.

Digital mark is a cryptographic worth that is determined from the data and a secret key known uniquely by the underwriter.

In genuine world, the collector of message needs affirmation that the message has a place with the sender and he ought not have the option to renounce the beginning of that message. This necessity is significant in business applications, since probability of an argument about traded data is extremely high.

Model of Digital Signature

As referenced before, the digital mark conspire depends on public key cryptography. The model of digital mark conspire is delineated in the accompanying outline −

The accompanying focuses clarify the whole procedure in detail −

Every individual receiving this plan has a public-private key pair.

By and large, the key sets utilized for encryption/decryption and marking/confirming are extraordinary. The private key utilized for marking is alluded to as the mark key and the public key as the check key.

Underwriter takes care of data to the hash work and produces hash of data.

Hash worth and mark key are then taken care of to the mark algorithm which creates the digital mark on given hash. Mark is added to the data and afterward both are sent to the verifier.

Verifier takes care of the digital mark and the confirmation key into the check algorithm. The check algorithm gives some an incentive as yield.

Verifier additionally runs same hash work on got data to produce hash esteem.

For confirmation, this hash worth and yield of check algorithm are looked at. In view of the examination result, verifier chooses whether the digital mark is legitimate.

Since digital mark is made by 'private' key of endorser and nobody else can have this key; the underwriter can't disavow marking the data in future.

It ought to be seen that as opposed to marking data legitimately by marking algorithm, typically a hash of data is made. Since the hash of data is a one of a kind portrayal of data, it is adequate to sign the hash instead of data. The most significant explanation of utilizing hash rather than data straightforwardly for marking is effectiveness of the plan.

Let us accept RSA is utilized as the marking algorithm. As talked about in public key encryption section, the encryption/marking process utilizing RSA includes particular exponentiation. Marking enormous data through measured exponentiation is computationally costly and tedious. The hash of the data is a moderately little summary of the data, henceforth marking a hash is more effective than marking the whole data.

Significance of Digital Signature

Out of every single cryptographic crude, the digital mark utilizing public key cryptography is considered as significant and valuable device to accomplish data security.

Aside from capacity to give non-denial of message, the digital mark additionally gives message authentication and data respectability. Let us quickly perceive how this is accomplished by the digital mark –

Message authentication – When the verifier approves the digital mark utilizing public key of a sender, he is guaranteed that mark has been made uniquely by sender who have the relating secret private key and nobody else.

Data Integrity – on the off chance that an assailant approaches the data and changes it, the digital mark check at recipient end comes up short. The hash of changed data and the yield gave by the check algorithm won't coordinate. Consequently, beneficiary can securely deny the message expecting that data uprightness has been ruptured.

Non-denial – Since it is accepted that solitary the endorser has the information on the mark key, he can just make one of a kind mark on a given data. In this way the collector can introduce data and the digital mark to an outsider as proof if any question emerges later on.

By adding public-key encryption to digital mark conspire, we can make a cryptosystem that can give the four basic components of security to be specific – Privacy, Authentication, Integrity, and Non-revocation.

Encryption with Digital Signature

In numerous digital communications, it is attractive to trade an encoded messages than plaintext to accomplish privacy. In public key encryption conspire, a public (encryption) key of sender is accessible in open space, and thus anybody can parody his personality and send any scrambled message to the collector.

This makes it basic for clients utilizing PKC for encryption to look for digital signatures alongside encoded data to be guaranteed of message authentication and non-denial.

This can documented by consolidating digital signatures with encryption conspire. Let us quickly talk about how to accomplish this prerequisite. There are two prospects, sign-then-encode and scramble then-sign.

In any case, the crypto framework dependent on sign-then-scramble can be misused by recipient to parody character of sender and sent that data to outsider. Thus, this strategy isn't liked. The procedure of scramble then-sign is increasingly dependable and broadly embraced. This is delineated in the accompanying representation −

Encryption With Digital Signature

The recipient in the wake of getting the encoded data and mark on it, first confirms the mark utilizing sender's public key. In the wake of guaranteeing the legitimacy of the mark, he at that point recovers the data through decryption utilizing his private key.

Public Key Infrastructure

The most particular component of Public Key Infrastructure (PKI) is that it utilizes a couple of keys to accomplish the hidden security administration. The key pair includes the private key and public key.

Since the public keys are in the open area, they are probably going to be manhandled. It is, in this way, important to build up and keep up a confided in foundation to deal with these keys.

Key Management

It's implied that the security of any cryptosystem relies on how safely its keys are overseen. Without secure strategies for the treatment of cryptographic keys, the advantages of the utilization of solid cryptographic plans are possibly lost.

It is seen that cryptographic plans are once in a while undermined through shortcomings in their structure. Be that as it may, they are frequently undermined through poor key management.

There are some significant parts of key management which are as per the following –

Cryptographic keys are only uncommon bits of data. Key management alludes to the safe organization of cryptographic keys.

Key management manages whole key lifecycle as delineated in the accompanying representation –

Key Management LifeCycle

There are two explicit prerequisites of key management for public key cryptography.

Mystery of private keys. All through the key lifecycle, secret keys must stay secret from all gatherings with the exception of the individuals who are proprietor and are approved to utilize them.

Confirmation of public keys. In public key cryptography, the public keys are in open space and seen as public bits of data. As a matter of course there are no affirmations of whether a public key is right, with whom it very well may be related, or what it tends to be utilized for. In this manner key management of public keys needs to concentrate significantly more expressly on confirmation of direction of public keys.

The most urgent necessity of 'affirmation of public key' can be accomplished through the public-key framework (PKI), a key management frameworks for supporting public-key cryptography.

Public Key Infrastructure (PKI)

PKI gives confirmation of public key. It gives the distinguishing proof of public keys and their appropriation. A life structures of PKI contains the accompanying parts.

Public Key Certificate, normally alluded to as 'digital certificate'.

Private Key tokens.

Accreditation Authority.

Enrollment Authority.

Certificate Management System.

Digital Certificate

For similarity, a certificate can be considered as the ID card gave to the individual. Individuals use ID cards, for example, a driver's permit, identification to demonstrate their personality. A digital certificate does likewise essential thing in the electronic world, yet with one contrast.

Digital Certificates are given to individuals as well as they can be given to PCs, programming bundles or whatever else that need to demonstrate the personality in the electronic world.

Digital certificates depend on the ITU standard X.509 which characterizes a standard certificate position for public key certificates and accreditation approval. Consequently digital certificates are at times additionally alluded to as X.509 certificates.

Public key relating to the client customer is put away in digital certificates by The Certification Authority (CA) alongside other applicable data, for example, customer data, termination date, use, guarantor and so on.

CA digitally signs this whole data and remembers digital mark for the certificate.

Any individual who needs the confirmation about the public key and related data of customer, he does the mark approval process utilizing CA's public key. Fruitful approval guarantees that the public key given in the certificate has a place with the individual whose subtleties are given in the certificate.

The way toward getting Digital Certificate by an individual/substance is delineated in the accompanying representation.

Digital Certificate

As appeared in the delineation, the CA acknowledges the application from a customer to confirm his public key. The CA, after properly confirming personality of customer, gives a digital certificate to that customer.

Ensuring Authority (CA)

As talked about over, the CA issues certificate to a customer and help different clients to check the certificate. The CA assumes liability for recognizing accurately the personality of the customer requesting a certificate to be given, and guarantees that the data contained inside the certificate is right and digitally signs it.

Key Functions of CA

The key elements of a CA are as per the following –

Creating key sets – The CA may produce a key pair autonomously or together with the customer.

Giving digital certificates – The CA could be thought of as what might be compared to a visa organization – the CA gives a certificate after customer gives the accreditations to affirm his personality. The CA at that point signs the certificate to forestall alteration of the subtleties contained in the certificate.

Distributing Certificates – The CA need to distribute certificates with the goal that clients can discover them. There are two different ways of accomplishing this. One is to distribute certificates in what might be compared to an electronic phone registry. The other is to send your certificate out to those individuals you think may require it by some methods.

Confirming Certificates – The CA makes its public key accessible in condition to help confirmation of his mark on customers' digital certificate.

Disavowal of Certificates – At times, CA renounces the certificate gave because of some explanation, for example, bargain of private key by client or loss of trust in the customer. After denial, CA keeps up the rundown of all repudiated certificate that is accessible to the earth.

Classes of Certificates

There are four commonplace classes of certificate −

Class 1 − These certificates can be handily procured by providing an email address.

Class 2 − These certificates require extra close to home data to be provided.

Class 3 − These certificates must be bought after checks have been made about the requestor's character.

Class 4 − They might be utilized by governments and money related associations requiring elevated levels of trust.

Enrollment Authority (RA)

CA may utilize an outsider Registration Authority (RA) to play out the important keeps an eye on the individual or organization mentioning the certificate to affirm their character. The RA may appear to the customer as a CA, yet they don't really sign the certificate that is given.

Certificate Management System (CMS)

It is the management framework through which certificates are distributed, briefly or forever suspended, restored, or disavowed. Certificate management frameworks don't regularly erase certificates since it might be important to demonstrate their status at a point in time, maybe for lawful reasons. A CA alongside related RA runs certificate management frameworks to have the option to follow their duties and liabilities.

Private Key Tokens

While the public key of a customer is put away on the certificate, the related secret private key can be put away on the key proprietor's PC. This strategy is commonly not embraced. On the off chance that an assailant accesses the

PC, he can without much of a stretch access private key. Consequently, a private key is put away on secure removable stockpiling token access to which is ensured through a secret key.

Various sellers regularly utilize extraordinary and some of the time restrictive capacity groups for putting away keys. For instance, Entrust utilizes the restrictive .epf position, while Verisign, GlobalSign, and Baltimore utilize the standard .p12 group.

Chain of command of CA

With immense systems and necessities of worldwide communications, it is essentially not possible to have just one believed CA from whom all clients acquire their certificates. Besides, accessibility of just a single CA may prompt challenges if CA is undermined.

In such case, the progressive accreditation model is of enthusiasm since it permits public key certificates to be utilized in situations where two imparting parties don't have trust associations with a similar CA.

The root CA is at the highest point of the CA chain of command and the root CA's certificate is a self-marked certificate.

The CAs, which are legitimately subordinate to the root CA (For instance, CA1 and CA2) have CA certificates that are marked by the root CA.

The CAs under the subordinate CAs in the chain of importance (For instance, CA5 and CA6) have their CA certificates marked by the more elevated level subordinate CAs.

Certificate authority (CA) pecking orders are reflected in certificate chains. A certificate chain follows a way of certificates from a branch in the progressive system to the base of the pecking order.

The accompanying representation shows a CA pecking order with a certificate chain driving from an element certificate through two subordinate CA certificates (CA6 and CA3) to the CA certificate for the root CA.

CA Hierarchy

Checking a certificate chain is the way toward guaranteeing that a particular certificate chain is substantial, effectively marked, and reliable. The accompanying technique confirms a certificate chain, starting with the certificate that is introduced for authentication −

A customer whose credibility is being confirmed supplies his certificate, for the most part alongside the chain of certificates up to Root CA.

Verifier takes the certificate and approves by utilizing public key of guarantor. The guarantor's public key is found in the backer's certificate which is in the chain alongside customer's certificate.

Presently if the higher CA who has marked the backer's certificate, is trusted by the verifier, confirmation is effective and stops here.

Else, the backer's certificate is confirmed along these lines as accomplished for customer in above advances. This procedure proceeds till either believed CA is found in the middle of or else it proceeds till Root CA.

Books by the same Author:

Search: "Simon Edwards"

at Amazon

Kind reader,

Thank you very much, I hope you enjoyed the book.

Can I ask you a big favor?

I would be grateful if you would please take a few minutes to leave me a gold star on Amazon.

Thank you again for your support.

Simon Edwards

Made in United States
Orlando, FL
04 October 2024